The Color of Faith

BUILDING COMMUNITY IN A MULTIRACIAL SOCIETY

Fumitaka Matsuoka

United Church Press
Cleveland, Ohio

To Dale and Dean

United Church Press, Cleveland, Ohio 44115
© 1998 by Fumitaka Matsuoka

Biblical quotations are from the New Revised Standard Version of the Bible,
© 1989 by the Division of Christian Education of the National Council of
Churches of Christ in the U.S.A., and are used by permission

Printed in the United States of America on acid-free paper

03   02   01   99   98   5   4   3   2   1

Library of Congress Cataloging-in-Publication Data
Matsuoka, Fumitaka.
     The color of faith : building community in a multiracial society /
Fumitaka Matsuoka.
          p.   cm.
     Includes bibliographical references and index.
     ISBN 0-8298-1281-4 (pbk. : alk. paper)
     1. Race relations—Religious aspects—Christianity.   2. Racism—
Religious aspects—Christianity.   3. United States—Race relations.
I. Title.
BT734.2.M28   1998
261.8'348'00973—dc21   98-26845
                                                              CIP

CONTENTS

PREFACE

How does race shape people? In this book, this question is treated theologically from the perspective of a person of color. U.S. society is not a harmonious blending of contrasting themes but is fast becoming an enduring culture of adversarial relationships. We are increasingly divided by race, class, and culture. The fear and distrust of difference rule our society, and this is often expressed in violence and brutality. On the other hand, Christians have historically sought ways to relate with one another based on something other than the idea that differences determine our identity. The community of faith is the community of those who strive to welcome "one another as Christ has welcomed us." For Christians, the matters of race and the ideas of individual and group identity need to reflect not only who we have been but who we are becoming. This book explores an interplay between race and the faith community.

The issues to be addressed are: (1) a theological articulation of the racial plurality in the United States; (2) ways of speaking about race and the enduring ignominy of racial pluralism; (3) racism as powers and principalities that monopolize the collective imaginations of people; and finally (4) existing signs of people coming together amid an enduring culture of opposition. Undergirding this book is my conviction that Christian churches continue to be witnesses to the vision of human community that breaks down "the dividing wall of hostility" in a racially and ethnically divided society.

U.S. culture is a very peculiar culture in the world where optimism is valued almost excessively. John Douglas Hall's description, "an officially optimistic society," aptly captures the prevailing triumphalistic cultural ethos even in the midst of disturbing signs of despair, pain, and violence. When this unwarranted optimism is applied to the perception of interracial relations, a dangerously distorted reading of reality perpetuates the racial ignominy and injustice so deeply woven into the very makeup of the society. And yet, faith communities of color have often persisted as the inheritors of a "thin" tradition of Christian faith. They do not shy away from penetrating into the shadowy side of life—failure, pain, and alienation—with courage and vision. This work is a modest attempt to bring into the open the witnesses of these communities acknowledging the limits within which human beings must pursue possibilities and visions. What has emerged from this investigation is a powerful expression of Christian faith in God, who is in solidarity with those who undergo the deep pain of racial pluralism—a God whose glory can only be glimpsed by those who in some measure are given to participate in God's suffering love.

Interdisciplinary in approach, this book is a constructive theological work that attempts to reflect on the role Christian faith communities play in American pluralism while forging a new vision of human relatedness and community building. The portions of this work derive from two lecture series I delivered earlier, the 1996 Stanley I. Stuber Lecture at Colgate Rochester Divinity School and the 1997 Religious Heritage Lecture at McPherson College, McPherson, Kansas. For editorial scrutiny and insightful advice for this work I am deeply indebted to Greg Loving, a Ph.D. candidate in theology at the Graduate Theological Union. Finally, my gratitude goes to Dr. Sharon Thornton, my spouse, who stood by me as I spent time involved in this writing— the precious time outside my personal and busy professional life that otherwise would have been spent with our family, relatives, and friends.

Chapter One

THE SPIRITUAL PAIN OF INTERRACIAL ESTRANGEMENT AND A YEARNING FOR A DIFFERENT WAY OF COMING TOGETHER AS A PEOPLE

Racial Pluralism and Theological Silence

Soon after the verdict was given at the O. J. Simpson criminal trial, Henry Louis Gates Jr. reflected on black indignation at white anger at black jubilation on the occasion of Simpson's acquittal. "For white observers, what is [as disturbing as] the idea that black Americans were plumping for the villain, which is a misprision of values, is the idea that black Americans didn't recognize him as the villain, which is a misprision of fact. How can conversation begin when we disagree about reality?"[1] How *can* conversation begin? Our pain is deep. Race relations simply accentuate the pain that is pervasive elsewhere in society. Our disagreement about reality points to the erosion of the foundational coherence of this nation. What was once intended to bring people together is increasingly becoming what divides us. Life, liberty, and the pursuit of happiness, once the unifying ideals of our society, are now the subject of disagreements, competing claims, and clashing voices across racial lines. We are alienated one from another in a climate of racial chasm. Conversation across lines of racial difference is increasingly difficult because the realities of life are experienced and understood differently.

1

Furthermore, the racial chasm reverberates with echoes of painful history. We are gradually reduced to silence. Where there is a loss of conversation, human life withers and dies. This is the deep spiritual pain of racial pluralism in the United States today.

The great challenge for our founders was to form a political body that brought people together and created a "we" but also enabled people to remain separate, to recognize and respect one another's differences. The "self-evident truths" were intended to ground both human equality and the power to govern by consent to "a moral order under a divine endowment of unalienable rights and a higher law."[2] Thus was born a nation, what Ralph Waldo Emerson called a "new race." But today the "truths" are not so evident and do not readily serve as the foundation for a harmonious blending of contrasting themes. This harmony that Thomas Jefferson once declared as "the expression of the American mind" is now full of sour notes. The "new order of the ages" (*e pluribus unum . . . annuit coeptis . . . novus ordo seclorum*) has included enough embarrassment since its inception—slavery, immigrant exclusion laws, and internment of its own citizens in camps at the outbreak of World War II, to name a few—that people who live particularly at the margins of society question its value as the convincing order for today's society.

The roots of American values, including religious values, can be traced to the American revolutionary tradition. The fundamental elements of this libertarian social system were democratic government, the Bill of Rights, a free economic order, and the security of property. This was a body of thought whose more exact origins can be traced to the leading Puritan thinkers. While the values appear universal, encompassing all peoples in our society, they were nevertheless forged to protect a particular group of people at the exclusion of large numbers of others.[3]

The theme of WASP ethnicity and superiority, which had been explicit until the nineteenth century, became implicit and taken for granted in the twentieth century. It was not until after the First World War that any really fundamental changes in the national ideology became generally noticeable. And not until perhaps the 1970s did the fact of U.S. racial pluralism become apparent. The fire under the melting pot went out. Protestantism and Protestant churches lost their near monopoly in the culture and are no longer in a position to dominate in acts of preference and valuation. It is within the emergence of national consciousness about the pluralistic nature of this society that racial pluralism and its underlying values and issues began to be acknowledged.

Racism, a system that promotes domination of the vulnerable by a privileged group in the economic, social, cultural, and intellectual spheres, has shown that the "truths" envisaged by the founders are indeed not so self-evident. John Adams declared that "the only foundation of a free constitution is pure virtue."[4] Our society today, however, is characterized by a cacophony of different and competing voices, each of them bearing a particular moral, cultural, and spiritual tradition and history. Each of these traditions is to a large degree alienated in its encounter with others.[5] "To be free we must be virtuous," declared Fourth of July orators.[6] Today a common meaning of freedom and virtue can no longer be assumed. What is virtue? Who defines it? What does it have to do with our freedom? People differing in race, culture, gender, sexual orientation, and ethnicity struggle with these questions. They view these terms in different ways, often in an oppositional and adversarial fashion because of their painful experiences both past and present. It is not easy to trust those who do not share one's common history and particularly those who are heirs of the inflictors of historical injuries. The erosion of trust among people exposes our society to the danger of being torn apart across the lines of difference, particularly racial and class lines, which breeds further estrangement one from another.

Such estrangement has a central characteristic: an absence of conversation, a loss of the speech that engages people in relationships. Silence and suspicion of others govern our societal life. O. J. Simpson has become more symbol than individual. He is every black man who has been pulled over by a white police officer, beaten to the ground, jailed without evidence, framed for a crime he didn't commit, or hanged from a tree in the hot Alabama night. Given that legacy, it is difficult for African Americans and other people of color who have been subjected to racially induced experiences of mistreatment not to doubt the police in particular and the intentions of the dominant society in general. Their doubts ultimately undermine the very foundation of our society. In such a time as this, how can we relate to one another across racial lines? Particularly for Christians, the question is, How we can honestly confess that we are created as one in the midst of our own racial differences? A significant theological challenge facing Christians is to discover what it means to live out our faith in a time when basic patterns of human relationship seem to be under major reconstruction.

At this time in our history it is necessary for us to pause and reflect on our race relations. Ideally, the struggle for the rights of each group is a struggle for the well-being of the whole society. Our concern is not just merely to record discords and cases of victimization. There needs to be a flowering of new cultural resources to move us beyond the increasing fragmentation and alienation among groups. The challenge is to move past a culture of distrust, a climate of alienation, to see in the dynamic of human interaction a new vision of human relatedness and community building, and to engage in action toward the creation of a just society in which the dignity of each person is affirmed and respected. Our challenge is not merely to struggle against an unjust society that stifles dignity. The challenge is to recover speech that permits communion with one another, to break bread together, a communion for which people so deeply yearn and we Christians confess to be our deeply held value.

Theologically speaking, the challenge is an affirmation of what Robert Alter calls "the quintessential biblical notice of the nexus of speech that binds [humanity] and God."[7] Our society must move from the loss of speech across lines of difference and alienation to a serious, covenantal conversation that fosters the root form of human relatedness: communion. "A [person] is truly saved from the 'one,'" says Martin Buber, "not by separation but only by being bound up in genuine communion."[8] Communion is not possible where speech is destroyed by callousness, violence, and other acts that erode trust among people. In the midst of theological silence, ways need to be found that open a world of conversation, communication, and communion.

In other words, we need to seek a way of relating to each other that we do not yet have or that we have long forgotten: a way of speaking about mutual relatability, intelligibility, and interdependence that goes beyond our captivity to the binary, adversarial, and oppositional discourse of human relationship. We also need a way of speaking about estrangement across racial lines that neither undermines the advancement in opportunities and cooperation that has been achieved nor falsifies the enduring reality of the injustices and poverty that continue to haunt many. Our inquiry seeks to move away from the divisive politics of race toward a responsible and just citizenry and peoplehood that respects shared values and differences and ultimately affirms the root form of humanity: basic relatedness one to another.[9] Envisioning such a "peoplehood" is a necessary theological task for today. The challenge is how to shape our society in a way that may reconfigure the racial differences that have long divided this nation.

The particular inquiry in this book takes place within a national conversation on North American pluralism and identity. The focus of the conversation is how people—differentiated and often estranged one from another by ethnicity, race, class, or culture—interconnect within the framework of society. Our task here is primarily theological. Our conversation is about North American racial pluralism seen historically and critically from within the actual lives and experiences of Christian churches, thereby animating an ecumenical conversation on our shared values and differences across racial lines. Why churches? Because they are the soul of peoplehood for a large number of people—particularly people of color—in the United States. Churches are the very embodiment of humanity for Christians.

The challenge before us is to:

- explore the common struggle of race relationships theologically and to assess the meaning of the Christian
  common confessional coherence of the Body of Christ;
  examine ways our society's values and institutions influence the manner in which group interactions have taken
  place and are taking place within churches;
- explore the ways in which power is used, held, and relin-
  quished in our racially pluralistic society and the means
  by which rights of racially separated churches have been
  balanced;
- witness to the signs of promise existing within historic
  faith communities for moving beyond the enduring culture of opposition and violence toward a racially just
  representation and community building amid our historically diverse and divided population.

The pain of estrangement and a loss of speech between human
communities calls for a theological response. The very foundation
of our humanity—our relatability, intelligibility, and interdependence—is in jeopardy. Christians need to know what it means to
actualize these basic expressions in the context of society's struggle to transcend its long dying.[10] Contrary to the current social
landscape, in which identity is likely to be determined by opposition, violence, and brutality to others (whether by race, culture,
tradition, language, wealth, credentials, sexual orientation, or
gender), the Christian response calls for an affirmation of community and the counter-themes of trust, mutual respect and the
vision of a new world. We "welcome one another as Christ has
welcomed us" even in the midst of our differences and painful
estrangement one from another, individually and collectively.
Christians confess that God's self-revelation in Jesus Christ brings
into existence a community, the church, which is called and
empowered to witness to God's intended wholeness and justice
for all creation. The church does this both by upholding the

vision of going beyond the barriers that divide persons from one another and also by opposing such barriers in the wider society.

At the same time, we need to be reminded that churches, too, have mirrored the flaws of U.S. society, flaws rooted in historical inequalities and long-standing cultural and racial stereotypes. Eleven o'clock on Sunday morning continues to be the most segregated hour for many Christian faith communities. An honest acknowledgment of the churches' participation in the evil of racism is a necessary step in the theological discourse about race. To engage in a serious discussion about race, we must begin not with the problems of people of color but with the historical and structural dynamics of U.S. society in which churches, too, are very much active participants. How we set up the terms of discussing racial issues shapes our perception and response to the issues.

The Christian vision embedded in the history of Christian faith communities is God's sovereignty, justice, and righteousness, which stands against domination and violence in all human relationships. Baptism into Christ and the celebration of Christ's presence at the communion table mark us as members of a faith community whose shared experience of grace is stronger than any dissimilarities or disruption of trust among us. This is the "memory of the future," the vision of the church's essential nature toward which we live. This vision of what can and should be is the measure by which our life as church members is judged. God's sovereignty stands against any oppositional dynamic as we relate to each other. Our collective and communal memory of the future points us toward a particular understanding of human relationship, a responsible relationship based on mutual respect, caring, and interdependence.

Theologically, Christians look for a way of relating to one another that is based on something other than the idea that differences and opposition determine our identity. We seek a new vision of community building in the midst of increasingly messy, fluid, and often strained relationships. To live in blessed communion is a serious and central promise of the gospel. To do so requires a careful and attentive examination of the interactions among racially differentiated churches and the ways in which society's values influence interactions among them. Our Christian affirmation of blessed communion, in other words, is expressed in the midst of the erosion of "communal" experiences of human relationships. We Christians come to the communion table in our yearning, hollow in our loss, to see if there is any speech and act that can take us again into communion that is genuinely blessed, communion for which we have been made, and in which we may live in freedom. This work is an attempt to explore the actual embodiment of such yearnings witnessed by Christian communities in the arena of contemporary race relations.

In order for such a task to be undertaken, people of faith need to be cautioned against easy reductionism of liberal "good causes," or pious romanticism, or conservative moralism, all of which cover over the violence, hurt, and pain experienced by people of color. It is necessary to realize that the legislative progress made in race relations in the past few decades still does not address the fundamental issue of race relations, which is the difficulty of trusting each other across racial lines because of a basic propensity toward evil that is deeply ingrained in human beings both individually and collectively. We need also to be reminded that for the dominant racial group the church's loss of its nerve and faithfulness is a massive, perhaps decisive, contribution to the brutality for which we have no adequate language. Today's crisis in race relations, with its violent and oppositional dynamics, requires a faithful living-through. That living-through is possible, however, only when the pathos of "peoplehood," the rawness of power, and the hidden resilience of God's providence converge. Without these ingredients, the life of faith is thinly deceptive.

The Actuality of Interracial Estrangement Today

The place to begin our conversation on race is with a critical examination of the American republic and its underlying values. Today the American republic, with its appeal to the abstract universality of inalienable rights, has become a place of encounter for rival and often mutually distrusting outlooks and experiences. In our racial scene, the societal coherence intended by the Founders is becoming more and more difficult to achieve. The doctrine of the "new race," that definitional and institutional ploy for a cohesive human community, has fallen short of its bright promises for many underrepresented people. This trend is taking place in the wider context of a world that is itself experiencing a massive, convulsive ingathering of peoples. Tribal warfare marks the global scene in postcolonial and neonational times. Even in religion, fundamentalists and extremists often outpace ecumenical and more tolerant groups. In the United States, the multiplicity of ethnic groups—European Americans, African Americans, Native Americans, Latino Americans, Pacific Americans, Middle Eastern Americans, and Asian Americans—has become a political reality and a cultural stereotype, however mythic their boundaries may be. These centripetal forces of group ingathering are at work precisely at a time when equally powerful economic and ecological forces demand integration and uniformity and mesmerize the world with a market economy, instantaneous communication, and rapidly growing technology. The world is falling precipitately apart and coming reluctantly together at the very same moment.

This has a profound effect upon the racial scene in the United States. Each racial group is increasingly fissured from within. Never before have so many people of color done so well. And never before have so many of them done so poorly, notes Henry Louis Gates Jr.[11] The realities of race affect groups in different ways. To compound the complexity of the societal landscape, the recent O. J. Simpson trials revealed perhaps the most basic and disturbing issue facing this society: people see life and reality radically differently depending on social, cultural, and racial location. We are only beginning to recognize that in a fundamental sense we live in different worlds, or "interstitial spaces"—parallel universes. Maya Angelou characterizes the Simpson criminal trial as an exercise in "minstrelsy": "Minstrel shows caricatured every aspect of the black man's life, beginning with his sexuality. . . . They portrayed the black man as devoid of all sensibilities and sensitivities. They minimized and diminished the possibility of familial love. And that is what the trial is about. Not just the prosecution but everybody seemed to want to show him as other than a normal human being. Nobody let us just see a man."[12]

In a less-publicized incident in 1991, four Vietnamese youths armed with pistols stormed into a Good Guys electronics store in Sacramento, California, and held forty-one people hostage. Speaking heavily accented and broken English, they demanded a helicopter to fly to Thailand and fight the Viet Cong, $4 million, four bulletproof vests, and forty pieces of thousand-year-old ginseng root. Eventually, three of them were killed and the fourth seriously wounded by a SWAT team. A spokesperson for the sheriff's department described the youths as "attempting to gain notoriety, attention and, perhaps, some transportation out of the country."[13] Reporting on this incident, a Vietnamese American writer had a radically different reading of the incident. What seemed to be a bizarre act from a conventional American cultural perspective was indeed an act of filial piety: "I imagine the Nguyen brothers adoring their father, the ex-sergeant of the South Vietnamese army. They must have loved and trusted his war stories. . . . The Nguyen brothers had folded their arms, the Vietnamese filial pious gesture, and asked their parents for permission to leave the house that fateful day. This image haunts me. They tried to bring dignity to their father by fighting his war. They coveted being good Vietnamese sons: To assuage the old man's grief, the young man must defeat his old man's enemy."[14] How can conversation begin when we disagree about reality? Reality is understood differently depending upon one's formation, history, and experience, thus deepening the difficulty of conversation across lines of difference.

Contributing to the loss of speech and deepening of silence across racial lines is the pervasiveness of radical individualism. Radical individualism has manifested itself in a very ugly fashion in today's race relations.[15] In the isolation of individual cocoons, we are no longer able to imagine a real-life, responding other with a center of its own. We imagine that reality includes only those with whom we share similar backgrounds, values, worldviews, perceptions, and cravings. In such a collapsed world there is no real speech because there is no one but us like-minded people, no one to address, no one to answer, no one to whom to speak seriously, no one who addresses us with authority. We are seduced into being alone within our small cocoon, alone with our wishes and cravings, but also alone with our hopes and our fears, alone in our silence, without speech. How can we engage in a conversation in such a world of subjective consciousness when we disagree so fundamentally about reality? Emerson's vision of a "New Race" is no longer a useful vision to guide us into the future in such a world of atomic fragmentation. The more such a vision distorts our collective experience of reality, the less useful it becomes.

This failure of communication and therefore the erosion of relationship within our society has also to do with the inability to acknowledge historically developed patterns of violent and destructive relationships, patterns of domination and subjugation that haunt intergroup relations and conversations. The failure is particularly acute on the American racial landscape. Even a cursory examination of our society reveals the magnitude of racial strife. "When it comes to the residue from our racial history, ain't nobody clean," says Spencer Perkins.[16] Evil is spread all over the board. The untamed, eager brutishness is part of what this society is. We have always been close to blood, either as perpetrator or victim, in both cases overwhelmed by a violence and its resultant estrangement that we can neither justify nor deny and that we mostly leave unacknowledged. The pain of violence is apparent when one looks, for example, at the experiences of Asian immigrants, an often neglected group in society. "Where once we had been lively, upper-middle-class families in that tropical country so far away, here we were mousy, impoverished, miserable exiles living in a deep, dark hole," writes Vietnamese American writer Andrew Lam.[17] "I wanted to make riches to bring back to my family," says a

Chinatown bachelor who congregates at Portsmouth Square in the heart of San Francisco's Chinatown, "but America is full of deceptions." These words reveal the prejudice, racism, isolation, and brutal power of violence suffered by Asian immigrants in racist American society. Searching for a better life, many traded hardship at home for misery in America.

These voices and countless similar voices reveal that people of color are not readily provided a public platform to express their suffering and injustice within a racist society. Neglect, misunderstanding, and at times concealment are often the case for race matters. For instance, the impact of the war in Indochina upon the refugees is just beginning to be understood: "As for the Vietnamese child," writes Andrew Lam, "at some point he comes to the brutal realization that 'his' side has lost, and 'his' nation is gone; that his parents are inarticulate fools in a new country called America, and he must face the outside world alone."[18] Even the impact of the Korean conflict and World War II on the recent Korean immigrants into the United States, particularly as manifested in their intergenerational relationships, is yet to be explored. The internment experience of Japanese Americans is also just beginning to be understood, primarily by the initiatives of *Sansei* (third-generation Japanese Americans) and informed *Nisei* (second-generation Japanese Americans). "In many respects the *Nisei* have been permanently altered in their attitudes, both positively and negatively, in regard to their identification with the values of their bicultural heritage; or they remain confused or even injured by the traumatic experience," says Nobu Miyoshi.[19]

The emerging pictures are disturbing. The scars and sometimes still-open wounds of these historical injuries are very visible not only in the lives of those who underwent them but also in the lives of subsequent generations who inherit the scars. For example, for Japanese Americans, who were racially and culturally isolated at an acutely vulnerable time in their history, the internment experience intensified a complex set of factors in their relationship with the dominant European American groups for generations to come. Suspicion, anger, and distrust make up one pattern of response.

Withdrawal, envy, and co-option are others. Some Asian Americans are accused by their own people of being "virtual whites." They are the ones who profess virtues that they do not respect, who secure the advantage of seeming to be what they despise. "What's irksome about the Asian American meritocrats," says E. G. Satiriko, "is that they give Asians, in general, a false sense of equality. Are we equal? Tell that to the Asians who are stuck in middle management and hit their heads daily on the proverbial 'glass ceiling.' "[20] A healthy and coequal relationship between Asian Americans and the culturally dominant Americans still awaits further healing of the wounds caused by the internment experiences and other historical injuries. Alienation across the Asian–Anglo/European divide, however, is only part of the problem. Deep-seated hostility and suspicion among Asian Americans themselves—for example, of Korean, Taiwanese, and Chinese immigrants against Japanese and Japanese Americans—have not been adequately understood. Interethnic animosity among Asian immigrants runs deep, sometimes even deeper than dominant-minority relationships. Here, too, an absence of conversation, a loss of speech, prevails.

The disturbing picture that has emerged is this: Racial identity is infused with a particular ethnic identity in terms of shared history and often painful events, perceptions, and group allegiance. Alienation from other racial and ethnic groups is often a result of investment in one's own racial and ethnic identity. A potent source of group identity is the collective memory of past glories and particular traumas. Passing these memories on to the next generation feeds racial and ethnic animosity but also helps keep the group's identity alive. Past oppression by another racial or ethnic group is remembered narratively and sometimes mythically, as though the past were the present.

For Chinese immigrants in America, particularly those for whom the memories of World War II are still vivid, one collective memory that has persisted with freshness is the atrocity committed by Japanese troops in the "Rape of Nanjing" at the outset of World War II. For Korean and other Asian immigrants, the collective memory of Japanese occupation prior to and during World War II, focused recently on the experiences of "Comfort Women," runs deep in their lives. Painful stories of earlier Asian immigrants to the West Coast are also handed down from generation to generation in literary and other art forms. A second-generation Korean American woman recalls her childhood experience in Hawaii: "My mother had many maids in Korea, but at Kipahulu [sic] plantation she worked in the canefields with my older brother and his wife. I remember her hands, so blistered and raw that she had to wrap them in clothes [sic]. One morning she overslept and failed to hear the work whistle. We were all asleep—my brother and his wife, my older sister, and myself. I was seven years old at the time. Suddenly the door swung open, and a big burly luna burst in, screaming and cursing, 'Get up, get to work.' The luna ran around the room, ripping off the covers, not caring whether my family was dressed or not. I'll never forget it."[21]

These memories persist with such power because it is a sign of both group coherence and sometimes allegiance to share these hatreds of another group. If one does not share the stories or myths that breed suspicion of the others, that person is not acceptable to his or her own group. However, ascribing racial conflict to ancient hatreds and other forms of historical injuries alone is not accurate. New political forces often come into play that fan antagonism between people who may have lived together with a relative lack of conflict. A group is most susceptible to such political forces after they have suffered a major dislocation or a loss of their psychological bearings, with the concurrent destruction of old verities and meanings. "The White Minority Syndrome is a well-documented phenomenon. . . . They [people of the dominant group]'re blaming immigration, birth control, feminism, anything. They are losing their grip," says E. G. Satiriko.[22] The current "white backlash" against racial and ethnic underrepresented groups reflects the dominant culture's perception of its eroding role in an increasingly diversified society.

To be sure, there is a tendency to perceive far more prejudice to exist toward racial groups than is actually the case. The net effect of this misperception is to suggest a stronger consensus than truly exists for actions against racial and ethnic groups. The reticence of those who do not hold the biased view to speak out against those who want to attack another racial or ethnic group plays a major role in the escalation of bias. Their silence reinforces those who advocate an ideology that promises a brighter future if the group's enemies—another racial or ethnic group already remembered and resented for past wrongs—are destroyed, as in the case of the rise of the Nazis. Estrangement across racial lines deepens in the silence of the populace, particularly among the dominant group.

The historical injuries are further compounded by the systematic withdrawal of economic and political support from one of the most deprived and segregated portions of our society: new immigrants. This is particularly the case with racially underrepresented groups. R. G. McClellan in *The Golden State* (1876) declared that "if society must have 'mudsills,' it is certainly better to take [laborers] from a race [Chinese in this case] which would be benefitted by even that position in a civilized community, than subject a portion of our own race to a position which they have outgrown."[23] Racism also breeds class differences. The "mudsill," the bottom of the totem pole in the societal hierarchy, is not limited to a racially underrepresented group such as Chinese Americans in its relations with the dominant racial group. Historically the presence of African Americans has in effect prevented the nation from being balkanized. "I feel personally sorrowful about black-white relations a lot of the time because black people have always been used as a buffer in this country between powers to prevent class war, to prevent other kinds of real conflagrations," says Toni Morrison.[24] ". . . In becoming an American, from Europe, what one has in common with that other immigrant is contempt for *me*—it's nothing else but color. Wherever they were from, they would stand together. They could all say, 'I am not *that*.' So in that sense, becoming an American is based on an attitude: an exclusion of me."[25]

Class separation based on racism fuels a widening distinction between the "contented" and the underclass, which in turn further estranges people across racial lines. "The underclass is everything the contented want to get away from, and they have succeeded remarkably in doing so," observes Robert Bellah.[26] Racial imagery sometimes emerges as class imagery and reinforces the perception on the part of the "contented" that the cause of the economic hardships of people of color has to do with their laziness and ignorance. The underclass, according to the contented, is actually created by governmental efforts to help them. The Great Society welfare programs, for example, are often accused of creating self-perpetuating welfare dependency. Seen from the vantage point of racial/ethnic underrepresented groups, however, the underclass is to a large extent created by structural economic changes, especially the technological revolution in the communications and service sectors. In these changes the society is no longer dependent on certain groups of people, particularly those who are not skilled and educated among racial and ethnic groups. "The fact of contemporary racism is mirrored in the fact that white America can flourish without blacks," says Peter Paris of Princeton Seminary.[27] Racial perceptions and images interface dialectically with particular economic developments and material conditions, creating a correlation between race and class, deepening the gulf between the contented class and the more differentiated racial underclass.

Race and class correlation extends to the tension and estrangement among minority racial groups themselves. Profound debates are occurring in minority communities about the veracity of group entitlement. While the recent announcement of the Clinton administration changed the racial identification for the 2000 census, the current Statistical Directive 15 of the Office of Management and Budget, which controls the racial and ethnic standards for all federal forms and statistics, is a crucial focal point of the debate. Directive 15's racial classification system—American Indian or Alaskan Native, Asian or Pacific Islander, Black, White, Hispanic Origin, and Not of Hispanic Origin—is used to monitor and enforce civil rights legislation and a smorgasbord of set-asides and entitlement programs. (Under the new standards to be used for the 2000 census, the racial categories are changed to: American Indian or Alaskan Native; Asian; black or African American; native Hawaiian or Other Pacific Islander; white.) In other words, the numbers divide the dollars. Group-entitlement concerns are thus creating considerable tensions across established racial categories and raising the question as to the legitimacy and appropriateness of the current classification. Senator and Native Hawaiian Daniel K. Akaka, for example, urges that his people be moved from the Asian or Pacific Islander category to the American Indian or Alaskan Native category. "There is the misperception that Native Hawaiians, who number well over two hundred thousand, somehow 'immigrated' to the United States like other Asian or Pacific Island groups. This leads to the erroneous impression that Native Hawaiians, the original inhabitants of the Hawaiian Islands, no longer exist."[28] The National Congress of American Indians, on the other hand, would like the Hawaiians to stay where they are. American Indian tribes enjoy privileges concerning gambling concessions, for example, that Native Hawaiians currently do not. Issues of money as well as identity are at stake, contributing to a gradual increase in interracial tensions.

The continuing and increasing volatility of racial questions in our society suggests that current race relations still bear significant scars from the prior four centuries of racial discrimination and brutality. During those four hundred years an array of political, military, religious, cultural, educational, and economic institutions—many of which still exist—was bent to the task of perpetuating racial stratification.[29] The current backlash against the accomplishments of the civil rights struggles simply confirms the suspicions of racially underrepresented groups about the tenacity of violence, brutality, and vengeance in race relations. The recent rise of racial essentialism and identity politics adds to the pain. More racial groups in the United States are stressing what separates them from other groups, particularly from the dominant racial group. An enhanced racial and ethnic pride and assertiveness among historically underrepresented groups is not the only

reason for this. The deep underlying cause of their separation is the society-wide denial of the tenacious rift in trust across racial lines that has always existed. Racial separatism is a desperate but to a certain extent understandable response to the denial. The silence and polite smiles of underrepresented groups have been mistaken for contentment. Only occasionally when a racial incident flares up is a comment like "I never knew they felt that way" heard.[30] The society-wide refusal to acknowledge the existing deep estrangement among a variety of groups, self-defined or historically imposed, is perhaps the most significant reason for the rise of racial essentialism and the desperate desire to provide an alternative expression of communal life.

Furthermore, extensive interracial contact and interaction have created a complex and distinct blend of political cultures born in Africa, Asia, Latin America, and North America. There is an emerging awareness among various racial groups that this society has produced deracialized models of communal life that systematically understate the potency of racial hierarchies while locating both the oppression and the accomplishments of people outside the dominant race at the periphery of historical and explanatory accounts. Advocates of racial and ethnic groups point out that many of the people now calling for a "race-blind" society are political conservatives who are likely to have an interest in undermining the advancement of racial minorities. Since the dominant culture has much greater access and opportunity for education and economic advancement, color blindness in effect perpetuates its domination. Despite their vision of diversity and plurality, liberals have also imposed their own agenda on the matter through the act of "redescription." They may pride themselves on their ability to tolerate others, but it is only after the other has been redescribed to fit the image and expectations of the liberal that the liberal is able to be "sensitive" to questions of cruelty and humiliation. Perhaps the redescription is based on the liberals' presumption of human commonality, i.e., "the other is like me" and their unwillingness to acknowledge the radically different. The act of redescription is yet another attempt to appropriate others disguised as a generous act of sensitivity to the plights of racially underrepresented groups. In both cases, color blindness and redescription, the alienation across racial lines is perpetuated.

Appropriation of racially and ethnically underrepresented groups into the dominant group is particularly noticeable in the trafficking of knowledge relating to the authority of the discursive norms and traditions that govern society. Intellectual protectionism is on the rise. The increasing volume of racial and ethnic underrepresented voices has been perceived as an "assault on the life of the mind," "biological insiderism," and solipsist "exceptionalism" by established traditional intellectuals such as Allan Bloom and Leonard Jeffries.[31] Ignored and delegitimized, those of different racial, ethnic, and gender origins demand that the cultural and intellectual hierarchy make room for their intellectual interests and reflect population shifts in gender and race. "For anyone to deny us the right to engage in attempts to constitute ourselves as a discursive subject is for them to engage in the double privileging of categories that happen to be preconstituted," comments Henry Louis Gates Jr.[32]

Perhaps more than any other racial groups, Asian Americans have been susceptible to "de-Americanization" or "Orientalization." Asian American writers, however rooted on this land they or their families may have been, tend to be regarded as direct transplants from Asia or as custodians of an esoteric subculture. Thus it is incumbent upon Asian American critics to orient discussions away from exoticization and to ensure that the word *American* is not blithely excised from the term *Asian American*.[33] The purpose here is not merely to point out Asian Americans' desire for inclusion into the mainstream culture, nor is it a critique of the conventional bourgeois culture that has prevailed thus far in society. Underrepresented racial and ethnic intelligentsia purposefully align themselves with the long-dispirited, ignored, and delegitimized people in order to claim their inalienable rights to "life, liberty, and the pursuit of happiness." Self-definition is the main aim in the intellectual endeavor of racial/ethnic underrepresented constituencies. Such a movement is necessarily insurgent in character.

The very operations of power within its discursive endeavors are meant to diversify and redistribute the inalienable rights that have been long controlled and defined by the dominant culture. This challenge creates a deep chasm between the racially and culturally dominant groups and the rest. The racially underrepresented groups' subversive orientations challenge the traditionally dominant norm of both knowledge and cognition. For the racially underrepresented, what is likely to be valued and affirmed is specificity in space and time instead of the universal and abstract; the tentative and ambiguous instead of the permanent and certain; the embracing of the neglected and invisible instead of the enhancement of the powerful and visible. Intellectual assets for people of color are primarily a historically contingent and individuated phenomenon that have been learned out of their painful experiences in life. Intellectual assets are likely to be respected only insofar as they are enacted in life. Furthermore, the challenge of the racial and ethnic intelligentsia to the established intellectual guilds has often been polemical in challenging the cultural homogeneity and hegemony of the dominant cultural asset. Such a posture is necessary in order to secure an audience, a listening ear, for the racial and ethnic intelligentsia. This is particularly the case for women of color, who are constantly in danger of being ignored and delegitimized. Harold Bloom calls this posture "the School of Resentment." Bloom laments, "Instead of a reader who reads lovingly, with a kind of disinterest, you get tendentious reading, politicized reading."[34] Between Bloom and the racial and ethnic intelligentsia the gulf of intellectual assets is indeed deep and wide.

A discursive move from homogeneity to heterogeneity, from the permanent to the provisional, from the unified to the diversified, is fraught with the danger of a lack of intellectual consensus across lines of racial difference. In recent years discussion on this subject has been divided between those who claim that "the Master's tools will never dismantle the Master's house" (Audre

Lorde) and those who argue that "only the Master's tools will ever dismantle the Master's house" (Henry Louis Gates Jr.). The critical focus and the context for such discussion has been minority-dominant group relations. Both schools prefer to stress the interacting operations of race, class, and gender.

Alternative to these two discursive approaches is "minority discourse," which focuses on minority-minority relations. Its basic premise is that there are certain shared historical injuries that have created affinities among racially underrepresented groups that cannot be adequately addressed by a model centered on a hegemonic culture. Underlying this intellectual discourse is the reality of a deep divide over intellectual assets prompted by both the radical demographic transformation of U.S. society and the gradual recognition of the wealth of the emerging cultural resources of various racially underrepresented groups, particularly of women of color.

Noteworthy amid such a debate is the work of Ralph Ellison, who, though acknowledging the oppression of African Americans as an essential and irreducible fact of American intellectual life, nevertheless wages an untiring intellectual war against those who regard blackness as an absolute, who see in it a release from the complications of the real world. Repudiating all notions of a separate intellectual culture of African Americans, he proposes a view that the black identity is inseparable from "American" identity. Life for African Americans is a discipline teaching its own insights into the human condition. "I understand a bit more about myself as a Negro," Ellison wrote, "because literature has taught me something of my identity as a Western man, as a political being."[35]

Going Beyond Old Paradigms

The pain of racial plurality is indeed about ourselves. The O. J. Simpson case, the Sacramento incident, and numerous other less-publicized cases remind us of the liminal spaces in our society that point to a fundamental disagreement about reality. The jury system is predicated on the idea that different people can view the same evidence and reach diametrically opposed conclusions. When race and gender intersected in the celebrated case, however, the implications of this idea became starkly evident. Anglo-European women tended to identify with Nicole Brown Simpson as an abuse victim. African American women, on the other hand, pulled by competing loyalties, tended to see O. J. Simpson as a black man framed by the system—even if he had been indifferent to the black community, and even if they thought he might be guilty. In such a liminal space, how can conversation begin? What has been revealed in recent years is the formational differences among people, both groups and individuals, that produce differing perceptions of reality. The difficulty of achieving societal cohesion has to do with these perceptional differences of reality.

The words of Medria Williams, an African American psychologist, concerning the Simpson trial capture the true pain of racial pluralism: "Where does the allegiance go? I started off going with gender, then I had to look at race. When I see the attack on the jury, it enrages me. I dig my heels on the other side. Now I'm feeling defensive. This has been a walking Rorschach test. People are reacting as if it's O.J. when it's really about themselves."[36] To varying degrees, this racial version of *Rashomon*—diametrically opposed interpretations of the same set of facts—is being played out over and over again across the racial scene in U.S. society. We view reality shaped by position, experiences, emotions, and needs, with variations in time, place, and situation. An explanation from one position may be valid from that view; another observation from a different angle may have equal validity. The notion that only one view represents the truth is difficult to accept, unless we assume either that one has a monopoly on veracity or, more likely, is powerful enough to impose its point of view on the others, which has often been the case in our racial scene, deepening the interracial division.

We thus remain captive to an enduring culture of adversarial relationships among racial groups, rage and distrust, an existing binary relationship in which one group's identity is determined by opposition to and violence inflicted upon the other. Our racial scene is further compounded by the denial of its enormity on the part of many in society. "Large numbers of Americans don't believe that discrimination is taking place," says Karen Narasaki, executive director of the National Asian Pacific American Legal Consortium.[37] The public does not generally view crisis brewing in the subject of race relations. In such a societal climate, it is far easier to assign blame than to render justice on the matter of race. There is no common ownership of the issues related to race, only an oppositional posture toward each other or a romanticized notion of unity. The culture of opposition has deep roots in Western culture. Radical individualism with the practice of a subjective consciousness fosters a worldview that prevents us from imagining mutual relatability, intelligibility, and interdependence: a real-life, responding other with a center of its own. We imagine that reality is only us. In such a world there is no genuine relationship but opposition, suspicion, and distrust. As Alasdair MacIntyre has shown, the adversarial culture is manifested in both public and personal arenas.[38] In the public arena, radical individualism is visible as a "managerial" consciousness in which all reality is reduced to problem-solving. Speech and act become only modes of instrumentalism for the satisfaction of needs and the productivity of payoffs. Racial issues such as civil rights policies are mainly treated in the legislative arenas. Absent from such speech is any practice of commitment that may raise any critical question. In the more personal arenas of our lives, an excessively "therapeutic" preoccupation may seduce us into yearning for relations in which there is no sacrifice, durability, or responsibility. This misguided passion for escaping loneliness through satiating relations leaves us even more alone. The world is defined by one's subjective shaping of reality, a shaping that can never satisfy, nor lead to communion, because the partner is permitted no real existence of his or her own. Silence deepens in such a world.

Behind the practice of subjective consciousness is a yet more disturbing notion: the seething brutality and violence that have

Chapter Two

HOW DOES RACE SHAPE PEOPLE?
WAYS OF SPEAKING ABOUT RACE

The Enduring Ignominy of Racial Pluralism

Wislawa Szymborska, the Polish poet and recent Nobel laureate, captures the central issue of race relations in the United States: "We know how to divide ourselves."[1] But do we know how to put ourselves together? A common and shared life is the daunting challenge of race relations in our adversarial culture. We are all members of this society, and whether we like it or not, no matter what racial group we identify ourselves with, a common destiny somehow needs to be worked out in order for us to live together as a society. The question is how to approach this challenge, given a history in which the identity of each racial group is largely shaped by saying no to others. South African novelist Nadine Gordimer's observation about racial identity of Americans is instructive: "When you have been so long rejected, your collective consciousness tells you that the open-door, open-arms invitation has come too late. You gain your self-respect by saying 'no.'. . . How shall people find their common humanity? And how to live, in the end, without it?"[2] When the identity of racial groups is shaped by opposition to others, especially in a climate of fear, distrust, rejection, and violence, then a shared peoplehood is extremely difficult to achieve. "Why do self-respect, identity, rest on this ancient and terrible tragedy of white rejection of black?" asks Gordimer.

In contrast, black South Africans have a different starting point for their identity. "Over more than three centuries of oppression and racist exploitation under many guises unequaled in place or time, black South Africans nevertheless have had their own earth under their feet. Despite neglect in official education, their languages have remained intact as mother tongues. Their names are their own ancestral names. Nothing—neither cruel apartheid denigration nor liberal paternalism—has destroyed their identity. They know who they are. In relations with whites, now that everyone is equal before the law, they do not have to say 'no' in order to assert pride of identity and self-respect."[3] But for us Americans, our task of finding our common humanity, peoplehood, is a daunting task because our history is against us when it comes to the matter of racial identities. An adversarial dynamic in human interactions and relationships has been the primary foundation for our identity building. People of color in the United States have not been able to freely shape their own authentic identities. In this discordant climate of a refusal to be like "them," race has been defined and peoplehood shaped. Given this history of ours, how shall we find our common humanity? In this chapter we will explore the ways race has been interpreted and the ways the various definitions of race impact attempts to create a common humanity. Then we will explore the question of how "peoplehood" is defined theologically through the confessional understandings of humanity and creation.

The Historical Origin of Race

People have either authentic or only imaginary ties to a common place of origin, noted Max Weber. "Almost any kind of similarity or contrast of physical type and of habits can induce the belief that a tribal affinity or disaffinity exists between groups that attract or repel each other."[4] Weber's description of racial consciousness is furthermore marked by another factor, a claim for "chosenness" that accompanies the racial superiority of certain groups of people. The "chosenness" is a violence-filled expression of status differentiation. "The idea of a chosen people derives its popularity from the fact that it can be claimed to an equal degree by any and every member of the mutually despising groups," Weber points out.[5] The concept of race as the framework of ranked categories segmenting the human population was originally developed by western Europeans following their global expansion beginning in the 1400s. Their self-definition of "chosenness" fostered exploitation and conquest of "others," those whom the powerful western Europeans attempted to subjugate, often by violent means.

In the United States, the systemic forces that sustained the forces of the "chosen" consciousness of Anglo-European immigrants gained their impetus from what George M. Frederickson terms the "status anxieties generated by a competitive society."[6] Particularly for Anglo-European immigrants who "had little chance to realize the American dream of upward mobility, it was comforting to think there was a clearly defined out-group that was even lower in the society Hierarchy."[7] In the South especially, the argument was that the social order should be based on a natural law that placed the master class in positions of power and responsibility. In recent decades there has been a reemergence of various white supremacist groups whose view of race is based on this assumption. At certain moments in our history they have coalesced, challenging the stated philosophical foundations of U.S. society.

The increasingly difficult economic, global, and political realities of the latter part of this century were the particular catalyst for the formation of a new phase of the far-right movement, which would come to be known as the Fifth Era.[8] This new age would see the creation of "an America Christian and masculine in its culture, racially white, English-speaking, and overseen by its sacred compact, the United States Constitution."[9]

The ideological basis for the notion of "the chosen" in the United States is distinctly religious in orientation. It is indeed called Christian identity. This ideology is embraced by some fundamentalist but less overtly racist religious communities. The origins of this Christian identity are difficult to locate. Some scholars trace its origins to the 1840 publication of *Our Israelitish Origin*, written by the Scotsman John Wilson. Another possible source is the Englishman Edward Hine in his book *Identification of the British Nation with Lost Israel*, written in 1871. The common element in both instances was the search for the lost tribes of Israel. The conclusion of both books provided the basis for the doctrine of Christian identity.[10] This identity theology with its two-seed theory—whites descended from Adam and Eve and Jews from Satan and Eve—became a viable alternative for disaffected fundamentalists. They gave to identity theology a racist cast directed not only toward Jews but also toward African Americans and other people of color. A curious exception in this identity theology is Native Americans. For some reason, they were treated as the origin of the white European race. Nevertheless, identity theology gave refuge to fundamentalists who could not understand the support given to the state of Israel by some prominent Christian leaders. Gradually the "chosen" consciousness undergirded by the identity theology provided the framework of the basic thrust of race perceptions in the eyes of the disfranchised white populace in the United States.

"Chosenness" thus served as an absolutization of the status of this particular group of people in the form of white supremacy. Chosenness is a powerful expression of idolatry. It is an act of rejecting one's own limitations and finitude and of giving one's own culture infinite significance. When a particular culture is taken to be absolute, idolatry emerges. Theologically speaking, central to the question of race has been the human propensity to elevate one group's particular historical development, "chosenness," over that of other groups or communities. This attitude of mastery causes other groups to be commodified—that is, treated as commodities—in relationship to the dominating group. When we fail to enter into relation with others as persons and not things, the distance between the groups thickens and solidifies. This failure to enter into relation corresponds to what Buber terms the "I-It" relationship, and distance becomes the presupposition for human encounter. Entering into relationship is an act of being human, and it is an act that must be repeated in every new situation. Distance, in contrast, is not an inherently human act, and neither is failure to enter into relation. "Distance" and "relation" are ontological terms for what constitutes being human.

The tragic result of white supremacy, an absolutization of one group's own history, is the inevitable self-enslavement to the very heritage of decay the group themselves created. We need to take note of Buber once again. Once distance is created through mastery, people enter into relation with others around them, able to enlarge, develop, accentuate, and shape the distance itself. Other groups of people become commodified. An end result in such a relationship is that human feeling disappears. Empathy is absent. In an I-Thou relation, people are capable of empathy, but the thickening by distance into I-It changes the whole situation of the other group, making them into an object, a commodity, and thus undeserving of the empathy that undergirds human bonding. Looking at others as objects, we make them part of an objective world with which we do not enter into relationship. Making an idol of one's own group ensues. One becomes blind to others' histories, the gifts they bring to the whole of humanity, and the experience of empathy in relationship. Theologically speaking, the holy is viewed as the One who is impassioned because God intends to be with people "showing kindness to the thousandth generation" (Exodus 20:6). The impassioned holy points to the fundamental way of the "I-Thou" relationship in the Christian confessional understanding.

Isolation and thus the dissolution of humanity are an inevitable outcome of self-absolutization. H. Richard Niebuhr points out the power of the historical context of human choices in *Christ and Culture*. "Though we choose in freedom, we are not independent, for we exercise our freedom in the midst of values and powers we have not chosen but by which we are bound."[11] In any general survey of cultural and religious values we do well to identify with H. Richard Niebuhr's insistence on the power of heritages. We may become so impressed with the heritage of our freedom and power and be so concerned to empty others of their own divinity that we shall empty them of their own intrinsic meaning. We become so much the master, so much in charge, that we sell people into slavery because of our program of expanding influence and mastery. A disturbing outcome is the spiritual malaise of racial supremacy, a malaise inextricably bound up with oppression yet not at all identical to the phenomenon of being oppressed. "Oppression is what the slaves suffer; malaise is what happens to the slaveowners whose personalities are warped and whose essential humanity is necessarily undermined by their position. Malaise and oppression are both painful but they are not comparable. The necessary first step in the cure for what ails the slaveowner is to free the slaves."[12]

Racial idolatry is the attitude or cultural ideology that lies behind racist structures and systems. It implies "systemic and self-conscious efforts to make race or color a qualification for membership in the civil community which was created by a particular group of people."[13] We need to see that the momentum of idolatrous tradition owes much to the great expanse of time over which it has been gathering force. We must ask what is our common fate as participants in this vast communion we call America, which has been built on such a tradition. We need to see that there are doctrines woven into the very fabric of our life and thought. There are beliefs or dispositions of mind and modes of response that we hold—even religious and theological doctrines we half-consciously affirm—simply because it has been our common fate to come into existence in that vast geo-cultural context that we call our own nation and society. Because of the idolatrous way our heritage has been shaped, we are simply not capable of creating a mutually caring relationship among people "showing kindness to the thousandth generation."

The decisive issue for our attempt to think theologically about race is the relationship between theology and histories. The unique and awesome truth about human history is that it can become creative or destructive, healing or hurting because at its foundation there is a mysterious freedom of human confidence and faith of the heart that can make both God and idol. An idolatrous life is one of the most dynamic situations that human beings can produce, but its product is paralysis and destruction, not creativity and life. Niebuhr stressed both the universality of the one God and the relativity of all historical manifestations of God and expressions of faith in God. When our deep-held values, images, and symbols point to an idol, then the critique of such idolatry must come from values, images, and symbols, or what Martin Luther calls "confidence and faith of the heart," which points to the true God. Thus "radical monotheism" sets the appropriate context for dealing with issues of pluralism, relativity, and a new understanding of the relationship of God and the world that comprise the theological task in our time. This is the threshold we must cross in order to go beyond the existing adversarial paradigm of race relations that has historically prevailed and to find an alternative, healthy, and constructive way of interacting with each other in society. Involvement in race matters inexorably brings people to deal with racial injustice. But what is uncovered as the struggle continues is the historical context, the power of our heritages, both secular and sacred, that deeply inform the very patterns of injustice. If the historical issues are not critically examined, the pattern of seeing others in an adversarial way will be likely to reduplicate itself. Hidden in the received tradition of the nation resides the dangerous assumption that liberty is earned by a particular racial culture and then doled out to those it deems worthy. This is liberty as idol. Idols are not holy. They are devoid of the empathy that creates and sustains relationship and community.

This idolatrous tradition of decay is deep-rooted. Jean-Jacques Rousseau raised the question: "What is the origin of inequality among [people], and is it authorized by natural law?"[14] In his attempt to answer this question, Rousseau postulated that the various groups of people differed mentally as well as physically. He stressed the importance of the environment in causing the diversity of people in different parts of the world, especially when the environment acted over a long series of generations. He then argued that unhappiness was largely due to inequality among people living in the same society. Hume, Kant, Voltaire, and others followed his path in speaking about race. Hume, for instance, stated that "there is some Reason to think, that all the Nations, which live beyond the polar Circles or betwixt the Tropics, are inferior to the rest of the Species, and are utterly incapable of all the higher Attainments of the human Mind."[15] Voltaire's statement on the characteristics of Africans was just as blatant: "Their round eyes, their flat nose, their lips that are always thick, their differently shaped ears, the wool of their head, even the measure of their intelligence, place prodigious differences between them and other species."[16] The racial labeling and ranking have varied in number, assumed precision, and acceptability over time. However, the underlying ranking of intelligence, attractiveness, cultural potential, and worth based on the idolatrous absolutization of "chosenness" of western Europeans has varied hardly at all. Race was largely viewed in its social ordering of perceptions, and this has resulted in the pervasive racism that continues to plague the world. This absolutization of prior histories and the idolatrization of one segment of humanity are perpetuated in every structure of society.

It is, therefore, necessary to historicize the concept of race if we are to understand its continuing significance in the present and the future. We need to understand how and why a ranked hierarchy of races that has been put to such destructive uses has been affirmed scientifically, challenged repeatedly, and yet still today tenaciously governs intergroup relations. There has been an enduring hierarchy of inequality, disparity, and ignominy among human groups historically expressed in the idea of race. This racial hierarchy, the absolutization of European history, is so deeply ingrained in the very fabric of our society that an exodus from its grip of power is a daunting task indeed. Economic, political, cultural, and theological enterprises dwell within and strengthen its domicile. The most penetrating way to understand race relations in this nation is to grasp this reality.

Slavery is the most blatant expression of such a racial ranking of people in the United States. To be sure, slavery occurred extensively in preindustrial social orders. What distinguished the slavery of the post-1400 racialized world was the use of racial identity as both its basis and its justification. In earlier slave social orders, the same physical types or culturally related groups might be either slaves or slaveholders. This shifted in the post-1400 western European racial order. The devaluing of Africans was shared by the western European colonial societies by the later 1600s. As the centuries of enslavement of these peoples continued, the economic uses of such racially ranked treatment were accepted more and more. By the 1700s, scientific efforts mounted in western Europe to place the exploited peoples into natural schemes that fit with their subordinate positions. One definitive racial categorization was established by Johann Friedrich Blumenbach. He divided people into Caucasian, Mongolian, Ethiopian, American, and Malayan races.[17] By the early years of the nineteenth century, theological debate as to whether these races were separate divine creations or divergent products of natural evolution marked the emergence of "anthropology," as the science of races was then called.

The historical definitions of race, in other words, reveal much about the value assumptions and worldviews, "the confidence and faith of the heart," of those who defined race. They also expose the structure and commonly held mind-sets of the societies from which the notion of race originated. The history of racial ranking was also manifested in the western Europeans' expansionist move into other parts of the world. Over the centuries Africa, the "New World," Asia, and the Pacific were encountered, renamed, mapped, economically penetrated, reordered, and politically dominated. The term "people of color" was thus redefined. It is not an exaggeration for sociologist Stephen Steinberg to say that "ethnic pluralism in America has its origins in conquest, slavery, and exploitation of foreign labor."[18] An end result is the stratification and disparity of people by these constructed notions of race, which established a deep-seated estrangement and distrust across the "racial" lines. The idolatrous history of one human group has become powerfully destructive, devoid of life-giving power in relationship, incapable of experiencing others' feelings.

The power of the idol manifests itself in the diminished well-being of those who are cursed by the idol. Interracial estrangement is largely expressed in the unequal distribution of rewards (those factors that increase control over certain groups and their own destiny, increase material comforts, and make life better), of power (command of resources), of prestige (social honor), of privilege (benefits, opportunities, and exemptions from certain obligations), and of wealth (money and property) to particular groups instead of others. In the process, the unspeakable pain and rage of those who have been on the receiving end of the racial stratification were rarely acknowledged by the dominating group. Estrangement across racial lines continues to deepen. Distance and opposition have become the basic framework for the definition of peoplehood. We must acknowledge the pernicious basis on which racial diversity developed in western Europe and then in the United States in order to come to an in-depth understanding of race and its significance today. Only in acknowledging the ignominy of our racial history is it possible to begin to understand why virtually all the nation's racially and ethnically disadvantaged people have confronted intense and virulent bigotry, why all have had to struggle to preserve their racial identities and institutions, and why the history of race has been fraught with tension, rivalry, and conflict. "American blacks want to stay segregated. And who can blame them?" says Nadine Gordimer. "The history of the country isn't theirs."[19]

In contrast to the effects of European colonization on Asia and Africa, the absolutization of one group's history took on yet another distinct characteristic in the United States. There was no large indigenous population that could be exploited by the colonial rulers in the United States. This dearth of population had different implications for the nation at different points in its economic development, and concomitantly, different expediencies were employed to secure the necessary population and labor. It was in this historical context and in the process of aggregating population that the nation came to acquire through slavery and immigration the racial diversity that is characteristic of our society today. It is true that groups of people entered U.S. society differently. Some came shackled to slave galleys, others on immigrant vessels in search of a better life. While such differences in the way people came to this society contributed to the complexity of interracial tension, an equally enduring factor is that these groups were used as disposable tools in the development of the capitalistic economy. "Like European overseas colonialism, America has used African, Asian, Mexican and, to a lesser degree, Indian workers for the cheapest labor, concentrating people of color in the most unskilled jobs, the least advanced sectors of the economy, and the most industrially backward regions of the nation," points out Robert Blauner.[20] This pattern continues even to the present time, with large segments of immigrants of color being placed in an unfavorable labor condition. Thus the "mudsill" effect of race relations emerged and continues in the United States with the powerful European American population further solidifying its own absolute position in the racial hierarchy.

Weber's notion of the "chosenness" claimed by the dominant population took the form of relegating people of color to the hard labor that built the agricultural and transportation infrastructure necessary for industrialization and modernization. What distinguished people of color from European immigrants were the barriers imposed on their upward mobility in the development of the capitalistic economy. While European immigrants "had a foot in the most dynamic centers of the economy and could, with time, rise to semiskilled and skilled positions," in contrast, people of color were for the most part relegated to the preindustrial sectors of the national economy. They were also denied access to the industrial jobs that lured tens of millions of immigrants from Europe.[21] To some extent, all groups began at the bottom either voluntarily or, in the case of African Americans, involuntarily. But the "bottom" or "mudsill" has by no means been the same for all groups.

In addition to the difference in labor deployment and economic function, the enduring inequalities of race also have their origin in the prevailing ideologies regarding people of color. Although prejudice against immigrants in general was pervasive across racial lines, there were some fundamental differences in the ways immigrants of European origin were treated and people of color were treated in this society. European immigrants were disparaged for their cultural peculiarities, with the implied message that they would eventually become assimilated into the dominant cultural group. The underlying assumption was, "You will become like us whether you want to or not." For people of color, however, the prevailing unspoken message was, "No matter how much like us you are, you will remain apart." Thus, the adversarial and oppositional dynamic of intergroup relations in racial pluralism began to develop on two fronts: At the same time that society pursued a policy aimed at the assimilation of recent arrivals from Europe, it also segregated people of color, who by virtue of their much longer history in the society had already contributed significantly to the shaping of a corporate culture in the United States. People of color were gradually silenced and marginalized by these two forces. Unlike other societies, where pluralism was formed out of a fusion of neighboring territories with distinct ethnic populations, pluralism in the United States evolved out of the displacement of masses of individuals. For transplanted minorities, torn away from their cultural moorings and lacking a territorial base, cultural survival would have been extremely difficult under the best of circumstances.

It is necessary, at this point, to acknowledge the difference in treatment of Native Americans and African Americans on the one hand and other racially disadvantaged immigrants on the other. The former racial groups met extreme segregation, sometimes even genocide. They had no place to return to; they were here in this racialized land, where they staked their claims to very limited territories, "reservations" and racial ghettoes. In comparison, immigrant racial groups had greater freedom to promote their special identities. They formed their own communities as a result. But given their position at or near the bottom of the class system, and their economic dependence on the surrounding society, they too were compelled to relinquish much of their cultural heritage in order to achieve their aspirations for social and economic mobility. In either case, this society provided only a very limited structural basis for racial preservation apart from an extreme segregation and genocide. The very circumstances under which racial groups entered the society virtually predestined them to a gradual but inexorable decline.

If we understand the history of this racialized nation with its propensity to erase the very notion of peoplehood for large groups of people of color, a propensity that continues even to this day, then we would also understand that the attainment of peoplehood, racial or interracial, is not an easy task. Nadine Gordimer's astute observation of the racial scene in the United States speaks of the vastness of our challenge: "black Americans do not want to mix with whites, however much potential comparability is beckoning to be recognized. The old, old answer I think not only survives but seems to have grown in bitterness, for reasons (of economics and opportunity?) Americans know best: when you have been so long rejected, your collective consciousness tells you that the open-door, open-arms invitation has come too late."[22] Historically, people of color have learned to gain self-respect by saying no. If we understand in depth that "peoplehood" as it has been transmitted to people of color resides in the historical and cultural matrix of rejection, then the reality of racial pluralism in this sense feeds the society's long dying, a dying it helps effect. This is the enduring ignominy of racial pluralism in the United States.

The Illusion of Precision: Emerging Questions about Race

Our racial scene is further complicated by the reality that there has always been an illusion of precision about race matters. Race is dynamic and fluid. The racial scene is always shifting, evolving, and ambiguous. Under the current census classifications, which have been recently revised for the year 2000 census, an increasing number of people of mixed heritages choose "other," a category that means different things to different people. The "other" category was created for people who didn't identify with the races listed on the census form, including people who identified themselves as multiracial, mixed, of Spanish/Hispanic origin, or Wesort (a mix of white, black, and American Indian found in southern Maryland). Nationally in 1990, 9.7 million people checked "other." This is nearly 4 million more people than the 5.8 million who checked it in 1980. The U.S. Census Bureau estimates there were 1.5 million interracial married couples in 1990, compared with 150,000 in 1960. In the 1990 census, about 4 percent of couples reported that they were of different races or that one member was of Hispanic origin. Such households had about 2 million children.[23] And yet this trend is by no means definitive. The May 1997 Census Bureau study determined that relatively few people would opt to describe themselves as "multiracial" on the census form if given the chance. And perhaps with the exception of Asian Americans, few racial groups would see their numbers significantly diminished if such a category were added to the census. This is so because the lack of precision and the changing nature of race have not diminished the propensity to see people in opposition, suspicion, and contempt. Racially ambiguous and mixed people continue to experience the pain of racial pluralism. The evil in race relations—that is, the distancing of relationship and the absence of direction for community building—has not been diminished by racial mixing. Is there any healing power as we continue to become more ambiguous about our racial identities? Will racial idolatry be countered in the increasing illusion of precision about race in the future?

Thomas Jefferson, who supervised the original census in 1790, divided the population into four categories: free white males, free white females, "other persons" (including free Africans and "taxable Indians," which in effect meant those living in or around white settlements), and slaves. The fact that nearly every government-sponsored census since 1790 has measured race differently is evidence of how unsettled this country has always been about its racial categories. Until recently, the peculiarly American institution of "the one-drop rule" was used to define a racial category, a rule that defined someone as African American if that person had as little as a single drop of "black blood." This notion arises from a long-discredited belief that each race had its own blood type, and was correlated with physical appearance and social behavior. This peculiar method of racial classification served the purpose of perpetuating the institution of slavery of African Americans. No one of "mixed blood" could leap over to the European American community— that was simply the predominant mind-set of the nation. "I think race is created in this country to separate black and white. I think of them as terms of war," comments Judy Scales-Trent, author of *Notes of a White Black Woman*.[24]

Indeed, historically, race has been discussed largely in terms of the black/white division in the United States. But today the increasing number and visibility of other groups—Hispanic Americans, Pacific Islanders, people of Asian and Middle Eastern descent, American Indians—have led to an increasingly multifaceted, ambiguous, and dynamic picture of race. The black/white relation as the basic paradigm of race is no longer accurate in our society. To the Census Bureau, the race question is intended to gauge self-identification, not give a clear-cut definition of biological stock. The last census listed seven racial categories: white, black, American Indian, Eskimo, Aleut (a native of the Aleutian Islands and southwest Alaska), Asian or Pacific Islanders, and "other." Hispanic/Spanish origin was considered an ethnicity. Under the recently revised census form, the government will allow mixed-race Americans for the first time to check off more than one racial category for themselves on the 2000 census. Under the new standards, people will be asked to mark one or more of the following racial categories: American Indian or Alaskan native; Asian; black or African American; Native Hawaiian or Other Pacific Islander; white. A separate question pertaining to ethnicity will be expanded from just the word "Hispanic" to "Hispanic or Latino," based on research showing that *Latino* is a more popular word in the western United States. The old policy of single-race checkoff came under fire after the 1990 census, when it was seen as out of sync with an America racially blended by immigration and mixed marriages. The very definition of race itself is becoming increasingly problematic.

But creating a multiple checkoff system is hardly a simple proposition. How far back does one go in identifying multiple races? Would one ask people to mark "all that apply" from a list of specific categories? And how will this system shake up data, which, in addition to providing a statistical portrait of the nation, are also used for such purposes as enforcing civil rights laws and monitoring housing discrimination? The multiple-race designation may lead to an overarching plan to whiten America. The multiracial movement, like the English-only movement and the immigration reform movements, is based on the mistaken premise that the United States has become a color-blind society where individual rights are more important than group rights. A multiracial checkoff system may indeed end up reinstituting the "mulatto" classification, moving the society toward a pigmentocracy where the closer one is to white, the more privileges one has. Furthermore, many African Americans and other racial groups are also of mixed race, and the multiracial identification has the potential for having a great impact on the number of persons who are categorized as black, Asian, or American Indian. Concerns are raised about its impact on civil rights enforcement efforts, which rely on the data provided through the census.

The issue is also complicated by the fact that some who might identify as persons of African American or Asian American descent may prefer to check more than one racial category because of their desire to acknowledge a familial heritage that is racially mixed. How would one define people without diluting the other things one believes in? More than anywhere else, the United States is in the midst of a massive cultural and social metamorphosis in its racial divisions. We need to rethink the architecture of race to reflect more accurately what is indeed taking place today. The challenge is to understand how race shapes people without stereotyping them.

Pacific Islanders and Asian Americans particularly are arriving at a crossroads. A generation after large numbers of Pacific Islanders and Asian immigrants arrived in this country, many have undergone transformations in how they think of themselves. To be sure, many Americans of Pacific and Asian ancestry still feel a strong sense of their separate ethnic identities, and ethnic groups still flourish in many cities. Yet the emerging racial consciousness is giving birth to many pan-Asian and Pacific Islanders' groups, particularly in large cities such as New York, Los Angeles, and San Francisco, where only in the last two decades have Asians and Pacific Islanders of different origins begun to live together. Talk of Asian Americans and Pacific Islanders as a distinct racial group grew largely out of the civil rights movement. In recent years, Asian American clubs on college and university campuses are organized increasingly around race rather than ethnicity. At U.C.L.A., about half of the sixty-five Asian American student organizations are pan-Asian.[25] Pacific and Asian American advocates argue that racism is the core of American society and that Pacific and Asian Americans must form a voting bloc to counter it. From New York to Los Angeles, Japanese Americans are the most integrated of Asian American groups. But they are at a turning point in their century-long history in the United States. The demographic picture is stark: not just a high rate of intermarriage, but one of the lowest birthrates in the country and a paltry trickle of about five thousand new

Japanese immigrants a year. Politically, they are still the best organized and most powerful of Asian American groups, with the
largest number of elected officials. But the Japanese American
Citizens League (JACL), the largest Asian American political
group, has been split by infighting between older and younger
generations as it gropes for a new, unifying purpose. While older
members want to build a legacy of the internment, younger members are pushing the league to become a civil rights group that
encompasses more Asian Americans.

There is indeed an illusion of precision about race today. The
idea that one's historical background, with the memory of historical wrongs inflicted upon one's person, will determine one's
occupation, taste, romantic preference, or anything else is challenged by an emerging idea in favor of one's perceived identity as
defined by class, livelihood, and cultural and political preferences. People of this society will find themselves surrounded on
all sides by people who are part Asian, part Latin, part African,
part European, part Native American. As the density of cross-
racial influences progresses, this society will get far beyond the
troubles the Census Bureau now has with racial categories,
which are growing because we are so bound by the barbed wire
of tribalism and because we fear absorption or "assimilation."
This reality has the tenuous potential both to force a reexamination of the entire concept of race as an irreducible difference
between peoples and to loosen the grip of racism in society. The
challenge is to examine how the increasing imprecision about
race definition shapes people in their interaction with each other
and, at the same time, to probe into the impact of the tenacious
walls of hostility that continue to exist across perceived or chosen
lines of group differentiation amid the changing racial scene.

Race is both dynamic and fluid, defying any attempt to provide
a comprehensive definition. Furthermore, each racial group, both
self-proclaimed and imposed, is so fissured from within that any
attempt to generalize its coherence and meaning is highly problematic. To be sure, the increasing imprecision about race does
not guarantee the emergence of a future where people relate to

each other with something other than fear, contempt, and condescension across the lines of difference. Indeed racial and ethnic groups within and outside the United States continue to stress what separates them from other groups. The May 1997 Census Bureau study found that the number of people who thought of themselves as being of more than one race was relatively small among all groups. For example, among African Americans, no more than 2.7 percent and as few as 0.7 percent of those surveyed considered themselves anything but African American, depending on how the questions was asked. Among Asian Americans, as many as 11.8 percent considered themselves as belonging to more than one racial category, and as many as 3.1 percent of these would opt to describe themselves as multiracial.[26] These findings might help assuage the concerns of some civil rights organizations that say a multiracial checkoff in the new census would diminish the official count of the country's people of color. They also seem to reflect the current worldwide trend toward retribalization. The fragmentation in which group is pitted against group, tribe against tribe in the name of a hundred faiths, historical wrongs, and identities is a tremendous challenge to every kind of interdependence, social cooperation, and civic mutuality. We continue to define ourselves by saying no to others. The essentialist definitions of human groupings often place excessive stock in fixed categories, ignoring the ways in which identities constantly shift.[27] Our society is at the very same moment creating separate groups and coming reluctantly together. This is the racial scene today. This is particularly true for the identity politics in regard to women of color. How do race and gender intersect with each other? Women of color are often expected to bifurcate race and gender, thus making it difficult for them to embrace the complexity and tentativeness of their identities. A common and shared notion of peoplehood remains a major challenge for us. How can we build a common humanity? The question becomes more complex as we enter a new era in race relations.

How Are People Shaped amid the Illusion of Precision? Perspectives of "Cultural Studies"

The recent trends within anthropology and "cultural studies" reflect some attempts to respond to this question. The proponents of reappraising definitions of culture within anthropology argue that the cultural history of humanity is not simply the sum of discrete histories of particular groups. People living together often do not share a uniform culture. Because groups interact in various ways—through trade, migration, or conquest, for example—the benefits of one group's cultural advantages spread to other groups even in the midst of destruction and estrangement. The interaction in itself tends to shatter cultural insularity, which can otherwise be stultifying: "We are trying to find our field in a seriously scrambled world that does not divide itself cleanly at the joints into societies or traditions," says Clifford Geertz.[28] A primary objective of this new direction in anthropological studies is to look at the dynamic of human interactions and not just to endlessly record human differences. The proponents of cultural studies maintain that in an interaction among different groups there is a "medium degree of tension" with the surrounding culture, but only a medium degree.[29] "When a changing culture poses new threats to established positions, it would be demoralizing to oppose none of these threats; it would be too costly to oppose all of them," even for a powerful and dominant cultural group.[30] What is often overlooked, they argue, is changes that have already embedded themselves within the membership of these groups.

Given such a debate on culture, a key question posed by anthropologists and ethnological scientists is this: Is race a legitimate concept for science? The American Anthropological Association passed a resolution in 1994 saying that "differentiating species into biologically defined 'races' has proven meaningless and unscientific."[31] While acknowledging the importance of race for cultural identity, the resolution says it is no longer a useful concept. A recent representative work on human genes, *The*

History and Geography of Human Genes, by Luigi Luca Cavalli-Sforza, is a comprehensive summary of the genetics of humans around the world. Sforza and his co-researchers say that the international genetic maps show that such popular indicators of race as hair texture, skin color, or facial features are superficial traits caused by recent evolution in response to climate and perhaps sexual selection. Tests of older, more reliable genetic traits, such as certain antibodies, do not divide humans into groups that correspond to racial stereotypes.[32] In other words, race is already close to being a useless concept in physical anthropology.

However, those who support the study of race argue that because scientists don't understand it yet doesn't mean that they should give up on the idea of race. The visible differences between different populations of the world indicate that race has some significance. While in science race may not signify much, in the social sense race is indeed a reality. In a collection of essays written between 1913 and 1944, Robert Ezra Park provided a classic statement of the major social forces influencing the way people interact. Park's intent was to debunk the idea that race as a biological concept could explain anything meaningful about race relations. Instead of the biological notion of race, Park introduced the significance of "racial uniforms" that are associated with the way race is perceived in the United States. Park's insights on race are reaffirmed today. Even anthropologists who object to the scientific use of race acknowledge that the public will continue to think in racial terms. Even with its increasing shades, color still defines people.

Thomas Sowell takes Park's notion of group culture as an important key to the group's social behavior and raises it to an all-embracing explanatory force: "Within all groups, important changes take place over time, so that neither their own cultures nor those of the surrounding societies in which they live remain absolutely fixed," he argues.[33] Park's emphasis on the flexibility of cultural values, particularly relative to race, is here transformed into a comparative analysis of various cultural groupings. "A particular people usually has its own particular set of skills for dealing with the economic and social necessities of life—and also its own particular set of values as to what are the higher and lower purposes of life. . . . These sets of skills and values typically follow them wherever they go."[34] Sowell's thesis is that the history of cultural differences among peoples enables us to understand not only how particular peoples differ but also how cultural patterns in general affect the economic and social advancement of humanity. He goes so far as to say that the habits and beliefs that a group brings to a new setting, what he calls their cultural capital, are far more important in determining their fate than the existing economy, culture, or politics within a society.[35] Given this reading of group interactions, race relations are seen to have a bright future.

Cultural studies generally view the fluidity of race relations as a positive sign as groups mutually influence one another, thus lessening interracial tensions. However, critically absent from this view is a whole range of structural barriers to advancement and opportunities for achievement for people of color due to the "racial uniform" factor. There are also those who argue that hard-core racial and ethnic consciousness seldom lasts beyond the second generation. Just as the Irish, Italians, and Jews encountered hostility at the turn of the century but eventually assimilated, immigrants from Asia, Latin America, and other regions of the world and their children can follow the same path if they try. Dinesh D'Souza, the Indian-born writer, says Asian Americans are already assimilating into the mainstream through education and entrepreneurialism. These efforts provide a quicker ladder to success than political activism based on promoting an Asian American racial identity. He considers this to be a uniquely American phenomenon. In other parts of the world, identity is not so fluid.[36]

Cultural studies on race introduce problems of their own. While acknowledging the illusion of precision about race, they also relativize group differences, sometimes ignoring the disparity in power dynamics that exists across the lines of human groupings. The particular vantage point from which cultural studies are considered exhibits a somewhat sanitized analysis of intercultural and power dynamics. To argue, for example, that slavery was not a unique Western evil but was a very common and widespread social institution in various parts of the world, practiced in one form or another in most societies, not only reveals a particular assumptive definition of scholarly inquiry into race—an objectified and relativistic sociological analysis that is itself a product of a particular racial history—but also raises serious questions of what constitutes an appropriate and useful way to discuss race in our society today. To view racial discrimination today as a rational response to generalizations about group differences, as Dinesh D'Souza does, is to fail to address the distinctive nature and deep sources of racism, which have to be addressed on their own terms.[37] Such an approach to racial concerns takes human and cultural responses at face value instead of looking at the material conditions in which they exist. Furthermore, it fails to acknowledge the tenacity of racism and the human propensity toward estrangement and oppositional ways of relating. For most of this century, sociologists and anthropologists have invoked cultural relativism to argue that all cultures must be judged by their own standards. Too often this has forced scholars to suspend ethical judgment. In recent years, however, some voices are calling on researchers to abandon cultural relativism and to become witnesses who record and react to events: "They must be willing to 'name the wrongs' that they see," says Nancy Scheper-Hughes, "and to hold themselves accountable when they fail to notice key ethical dilemmas."[38] The impact of such a shift still remains to be seen.

To understand the contributions and limitations of cultural studies on race matters, we also need to examine the forces of modernity and the value assumptions that inevitably impact such studies. Contemporary attitudes and ideas are direct consequences of living in a modern democracy, or what Allan Bloom terms "democratic personality." In spite of Bloom's controversial view, his thoughts on the nature of modernity deserve attention. "Democratic personality" has an unspoken absolute, freedom, and a primary value, equality. That personality, Bloom argues, must face a tension between the principle of equality and the idea of actually occurring difference. In democracy it is particularly painful to confront intrinsic differences in cultures, in abilities, in views, in possibilities. That tension is at the foundation of the culture wars. Multiculturalism posits that there is no objective standard by which one culture can be judged superior to another, thus enshrining the principle of equality. This leads to an exaggeration of the democratic ideal: ideas themselves have become distorted by being democratized. Nothing can be right, wrong, better, or worse, and no distinctions can be made. Beneath the conservative and neoconservative views on race by Dinesh D'Souza and Thomas Sowell appears to lie such an exaggeration of the democratic ideal. This is an inherently "modern" worldview, or what Lionel Trilling calls "a general enlargement and freedom and rational direction of human life." A real danger is its tendency to constrict its views of the world, simplifying them, denying complexity and often turning sentimental.

Critical Race Theory

Critical race theory is an attempt to demonstrate that there is no free market of race. Race indeed matters. "The time will come soon when we will have to come forward with new ideas about race," says Cornel West.[39] The recent emergence of critical race theory is a corrective to the more orthodox cultural studies. Critical race theory holds that people's perspectives on events are overwhelmingly determined by their racial background. Critical race theorists argue that there are competing racial versions of reality that may never be reconciled. They would argue that because few people in the racially dominant group will ever be able to see things as people of color do, real racial understanding may be beyond the nation's reach. *Rashomon* perspectives are what is left, making interracial communication practically impossible. Critical race theory is an attempt to bring race to the very center of the analysis of most situations. Its assumption is that race has pervasively affected our perception of reality and our understanding of the world. Originally discussed in law schools, critical race theory has spread far beyond those institutions to become a significant new front in the increasingly fractious culture wars. Critical race theory has a clear and obvious bearing on familiar issues like the legitimacy of ebonics and ethnocentric curricula and the fairness of affirmative action—helping to explain how people across color lines can find themselves quavering with exasperation at each other's views on various issues.

Perhaps most significantly, critical race theory provides an intellectual foundation for emerging forms of racial and ethnic separateness. The most prominent issue here is a reconsideration of the goals and success of the civil rights movement. Critical race theorists reject the classic liberal view of integration and assimilation as the ultimate goal. Critical race theory counters color blindness by saying that race is not simply skin color. It tries to reveal the ways that race is a social construct structured out of law, culture, and history. These matters—law, culture, and history—are not usually neutral. They are simply facilitating whatever power relationships were in existence when they were put in place. An example is the criminal justice system: Why are a disproportionate number of the men in America's jails black? Critical race theorists argue that it is because the system is infected with racism at every level.

Some critical race theorists say an important tool for underrepresented people of color in overcoming their disadvantages is to tell stories, either from individual experience or from parables. Storytelling aims at challenging versions of reality put forward by the dominant culture. An ethnic/racial person, for example, may tell stories about police brutality that are at odds with the official version of how common such behavior is. By putting forward an anecdotal version of reality, that person asserts the primacy of personal experience—and no matter what society tells that person, he or she trusts his or her own personal experiences. By telling a story, scholars of color have a distinct voice that rejects narrow evidentiary concepts of relevance and credibility. Some go so far as to say that what really happened in a particular incident may be no more important than what people feel or say happened because their voices accurately represent their collective fear of mistreatment, a fear reinforced by centuries of domination and subjugation. Critical race theory is an indigenous approach to racial identity building that is emerging among underrepresented racial intellectuals. It is a maturing extension of the intellectual movement that has roots in the time of slavery with gospel music and slave narratives for African Americans. Embedded in the oppositional dynamic prevalent in the U.S. societal framework, it is nevertheless an indicator of how to rethink the architecture of race. What we see in the recent scholarship on race is an enduring hunger for honest talk about America's continuing dilemma—the larger issue of race and identity in American life.

Speaking of Peoplehood Theologically

We need to remind ourselves that how race is defined and interpreted has profound implications for the credibility of an exploration into matters of race. To speak of race theologically is a confessional act for Christians. It is intrinsically related to our understanding of the creation and the role of humanity, both personally and communally. To speak of race theologically is to confess our finitude and the goodness of creation, sin and the promise of redemption rooted in Christian convictions about the nature of God, humanity, and church. It involves the risk of a confessional parochialism just as it expresses an eschatological yearning that is ultimately unprovable. There is no assurance of a just outcome in such an act of seeking, only the promise of "all things being made anew." However, to speak of race as a confessional act is indeed an expression of faithfulness.

Theology today is increasingly appreciated as having vitality and credibility insofar as its traditional resources embrace new voices and their differences in earnest response to significant issues. The emergence in theology of the language of crisis constitutes a discursive shift that attempts to bolster its credibility. To speak of race theologically is to analyze the deprivation of conditions of life and the possibility for human flourishing. It is an act of denouncement of sin and an announcement of grace in light of Christians' faith confession. The pain of fragmentation and estrangement across human communities calls for a theological response. If the fundamental confidence in the goodness of creation that Christians confess in faith is in jeopardy, we must know it theologically in the context of the society's struggle against the decay of life.

Contrary to the current picture of our society where one's group identity is determined by an opposition to the other—race, culture, tradition, language, wealth, credentials, sexual orientation, or gender—the response grounded in faith for Christians is the creation of "household" by welcoming one another regardless of differences. God's sovereignty—that is, God's justice and righteousness—stands against hierarchy or domination in relationships. It also stands against an oppositional and adversarial dynamic as we relate to each other. Instead, our collective "memory of the future"[40] gives us a particular way of understanding human relationship, a responsible relationship based on mutual respect and caring. Theology is a proper way for Christians to speak about race precisely because the theological enterprise grows from, and intends to flower in, new visions of "emancipatory praxis."[41] Theology takes part in reforming communal and political life within faith communities and through such a critical act also witnesses to the world with its particular perspectives and value orientations. Theology in this sense is very much public in character.

Theologically speaking, the very definition of race needs to take into consideration the question of what constitutes "we" in our society. One of the traditional responses to this question vis-à-vis race is a ranked membership in a population, either imposed from outside or affirmed from within. If this membership is self-perceived, it is essentially what ethnicity is all about.

Words of caution are in order. The conflation of the terms *race* and *ethnicity* needs to be avoided because of its possible undermining effects upon the hard struggles of racially underrepresented populations, however they define their racial identities themselves.[42] Arthur Schlesinger Jr. argues that the "cult of ethnicity" portends a dangerous new turn in American life, even a return to racial segregation.[43] Such an argument itself reveals a deep gulf that is developing between the dominant racial group and underrepresented people of color. The term *ethnicity* is here given a connotation of an objectified group of people that claims its own legitimacy in society. Ethnicity is indeed an affirmation of shared cultural values among a particular group of people. It is not to be uncritically equated with an act of entitlement claimed by the group among others in society. What distinguishes ethnicity from race is the "uniform" factor, color, which Park identifies. Ethnicity does not necessarily imply a racial uniform, whereas color is inherent in race definitions.

Seen from the perspective of racially underrepresented groups, "race" is an expression of a strong group coherence and a claim for equal opportunity and treatment of their peoplehood associated with the underlying significance of color, the significance in human relationship and historical injuries that accompany color. Divergent and conflicting perspectives about race between the dominant racial group and underrepresented groups are shaped by how each group thinks about color and the history associated with peoplehood. The varied perspectives on race illustrate how we know what we know about our past and how lopsided the relatability across races has been among various group of people. Different readings of history not only produce different readings of reality but also breed profound alienation on all sides due primarily to the imbalance of power and the resultant artificially binary discourse of accusation and counteraccusation, of grievance and countergrievance.

Speaking of public reactions to the Simpson verdict, Henry Louis Gates Jr. commented on the persistent culture of opposition in the United States: "The result is that race politics becomes a court of the imagination wherein blacks seek to punish whites for their misdeeds and whites seek to punish blacks for theirs, and an infinite regress of score-settling ensues—yet another way in which we are daily becoming meta and meta. And so an empty vessel like O. J. Simpson becomes filled with meaning, and more meaning—more meaning than any of us can bear."[44] It is emotionally more satisfying to place blame than to render justice. How do we move away from this pattern of human relationships to a paradigm that shifts the conversation into a new arena? This is the crux of the issue for race seen from a theological perspective.

Central to a Christian understanding of human relationships is the church, which is called and empowered to witness to God's intended wholeness for all creation. The church does this both by transcending in its own life those barriers (e.g., of race and culture) that divide persons from one another and by opposing such barriers in human society. Our baptism into Christ and our celebration of Christ's presence at the Table mark us as members of a faith community whose shared experience of grace is stronger than any dissimilarities and estrangement among us. This is the vision of the church's essential nature toward which we live and thus is the measure by which our life as church is judged. Peoplehood, in other words, is understood in terms of this vision of community. Community as a Christian experience of peoplehood is not optional; it is given in Christ amid the full diversity of peoples, cultures, traditions, races, and languages. Being people is not defined by a particular color, language, location, or gender. In other words, people are not defined by the way they differ from other peoples.

Scripture declares that Christians are a peculiar kind of people without national boundaries or common language or single color and cultural identity but nonetheless related by blood. Such an understanding of peoplehood is a radical departure from our conventional and prevailing experiences of race relations. It is perhaps almost inconceivable and becoming more so in recent years. It is a countercultural view of human relationship: "in that while we yet were sinners Christ died for us." The church is a particular and peculiar kind of "peoplehood" that responds to the unfathomable generosity of God by "welcoming one another as Christ has welcomed us"—hospitality not just for a homogeneous group of people, but instead for those from whom we are estranged, even enemies, all for whom Christ died. In other words, the foundational starting point for Christians in our understanding of peoplehood is God's gift of grace, which coheres all people even in the midst of estrangement. This is the framework within which the actual life of Christian faith communities has witnessed to God's redeeming love.

The signs that counter the currently prevailing oppositional dynamic of race relations in the United States are indeed present in numerous Christian faith communities in spite of their countless failures to live up to their vision. To speak about race theologically, then, is to witness to those signs of counter values that have been remembered, told, and reenacted over and over even at the "most segregated hour" in our society. Amid a society that holds up particularly constructed identities most cherished and polemically defended, the starting point for Christians is that we are whole people, not defined solely by our particular race. Particularity is a reality that cannot be denied but, in the final analysis, the accent in the Christian tradition is on relatedness. If the starting point is difference, then relatedness is conceived of as peaceful coexistence, and it lasts as long as interests are perceived to coincide. This is the pluralistic ideology of U.S. public life that often degenerates into a culture of narcissism and self-preoccupation in which groups retreat from public dialogue into what T. W. Adorno calls "private reservoirs of the spirit" whenever doing so furthers their agenda. Diversity, even estrangement, in Christian perspective, is a relational concept seen from the confessional notion of solidarity and mutual enrichment. It assumes the fundamental relatedness of all creation.

The decisive issue for the attempt to think theologically about race is theology's relationship to group histories. Alienation, displacement, and erosion of trust affect people even within a particular racial group as well as across racial lines as a result of filling our histories with "more meaning than any of us can bear." The pain is deep, ripping the very fabric of our society, intensifying the alienation across and within various groups and undermining mutual relatability within society. The increasingly ambiguous and problematic definition of racial categories merely contributes to the pain and the further diminishing of a coherent peoplehood. The illusion of precision about race does not ease the pain of racial plurality. On the contrary, it makes race matters more complex, confusing, and painful. Recent racial tensions in some of the major U.S. urban centers testify to this. And yet, there are unmistakable signs of hope that counter the prevailing forces in race relations. These signs, at least some of them, exist within Christian faith communities that continue to respond to the unfathomable generosity of God by welcoming one another. They may appear insignificant to the cynical and pessimistic eye, and they often prove not to be newsworthy. But they are powerful forces that refuse to go away in the midst of the current confusion, pain, and bewilderment in race relations. An acknowledgment and recovery of these signs is what is needed in order to go beyond the "infinite regress of score-settling" that persists today.

Before we proceed with our faith conviction and its power to address today's racial ills, however, we need to be mindful of the tenacity of racial evil at the very core of our society and its make-up. This is to say that any attempt to rectify the ills of interracial relations is likely to involve both provisional and stop-gap approaches, which do not speak to the basic cause of the problem. As Benjamin Mays states, "The nation cannot reconstruct that which it has not constructed." The very structure of U.S. society is based on the actuality that its national ideal—the guarantee of equality, justice, and the pursuit of happiness for all—was defined by a powerful dominant racial and cultural group and not representatively created by the various groups of people who made up this society. There is, therefore, an inherent inequality about the foundation of societal coherence. A

Chapter Three

RACISM AS A MONOPOLY OF IMAGINATION

Racism: A Negation of Relationship and an Absence of Direction in a Collective Human Life

It is the failure to enter into relation that in the last analysis constitutes evil, or nonexistence. It is the reestablishment of just relation that leads to the redemption of evil and genuine human existence. Evil is both negation of relationship and absence of direction for a collective human life, as Martin Buber reminds us.[1] Evil originates in the devaluation of a collective human life, inevitably accompanied by coercion and often violence. Every concentration of power and wealth is based on some kind of seizure by violence.[2] Evil manifests itself as powers and principalities within institutions in their function of mediating life's resources historically, publicly, and experientially. Evil is embodied within institutions that mobilize coercive social power, consolidate human knowledge, diminish life, and sometimes even mediate power toward death, and results in a "monopoly of imagination."[3] Evil acts as forces that claim both the sole voice in determining how things are experienced and the right and legitimacy to supply the lens through which life is properly viewed or experienced. Evil affects both the dominating and the dominated across the breadth of human life. Institutionally, evil generates images, metaphors, paradigms, and categories to which those who are in the position of dominance become captive. Those who are at the margins become suspicious and cynical about the possibility of a life together in the captivity of the dominant group to these images. Evil creates injustice that devalues existence and turns people at the margins into victims. It estranges us all by eroding trust in relationship and creating a deep gulf in communication, ultimately making the future less promising for all.

Reconciliation, which is the mutual mending of relationship, cannot be accomplished by merely tending to broken relationships or breakdowns in communication without rectifying injustice done to victims. Any discussion about race relations, particularly "to lift the burdens of race from our children's future," as President Clinton calls for, needs to take into account the impact of pervasive racism upon our very existence, both individually and communally.[4] Racism is sociologically defined as a structural and systemic deprivation of the human rights and dignity of people of color by those who are in positions of dominance. Racism is more than that, however. It is the negation of relation and the absence of direction for a collective human life due to the devaluation of life generated within societal institutions functioning as powers and principalities in our communal life. In this sense, racism is an obstacle to the formation of a common peoplehood. The negation of relation and the absence of direction are evil not because of some conceptional notion of evil but because of a total attitude expressed in both life and thought. This attitude is a mode of seeing and being that dwells in life itself, which expresses itself through forces of violence operating within institutions and interpersonal relationships. When life is devalued because of skin color, racism's impact is widespread, encompassing not only oppressors and victims but the whole society.

Racism as the negation of relation and the absence of direction in a collective life of people results from the devaluation of life. But the powers and principalities of racism do not exist as independent and autonomous entities created by a group of individuals. They are posited, curiously and inevitably, in the midst of our yearning for a new life, a "more excellent way," particularly among those who are the victims. The powers and principalities of racism are indeed parasites of the good, not having an existence of their own. The powers and principalities undermine our valuations and actions; but an act of valuing is nothing other than an act of freedom to choose what is good or evil and the posture one then takes toward either enacting evil or avoiding evil and even transforming evil into good. Evil is in one way or another recognized as having reality, even if only that of a temporary accompaniment of unredeemed creation. But its reality is never autonomous and permanent, nor is it ever completely divorced from the good. Hence it is a possible object of redemptive activity.

This is to say that righteousness and justice are always choices surrounded by fear, greed, hate, and revenge, choices often taken in great danger and at great risk, requiring not only nobility but trusting, submitting, and yielding to that which is good and ulti-mate. Righteousness and justice are powerful expressions that counter the "monopoly of imagination" by those who are not subservient to the monopoly. They are expressed as yearning out of the hurt of the evil of racism by people of color at the margins. Righteousness and justice are therefore speeches of hope that proclaim that new life is possible even in the midst of the over-whelming rampage of evil. Righteousness and justice are signs of healing essentially and powerfully embodied in communal activ-ity, with the neighbor being the proximate source of life. They are intentional public nurturing and communal images of an authentic peoplehood. An authentic peoplehood is a wistful longing for life that could be lived with a singleness of vision that is driven by neither violence nor fear, characterized by mutuality, directness, presentness, intensity, and ineffability. (We will wit-ness to signs of such a longing in the next chapter.)

Righteousness and justice as moral possibilities in the midst of the evil of racism are likely to be mediated through subsidiary insti-tutions in society that function in the presence of the dominating institutions, to quite different effect.[5] Subsidiary institutions such as churches, families, neighborhoods, and voluntary organizations keep their sense of freedom from and maintain a tension with the dominant ideological forces in society. These institutions challenge the monopoly of imagination not by coercive force but by patient persuasion, exhibiting signs of righteousness and justice in their own being and acting even in the midst of what appears to be a hopeless situation.

When one fails to enter into relation due to the coercion and violence of the monopoly of imagination, that is, the powers and principalities manifested in societal institutions, then the distance among people thickens and solidifies. Instead of being that which enables relationship to flourish, distance among people widens. Entering into relation is in fact *the* act by which we constitute ourselves as human, and it is an act that must be repeated over again in every new situation. Distance has an ontological quality to it that cannot be overcome by societal sanctions alone. Overcoming distance-as-obstructing-relation requires transformation, a change of heart intentionally undertaken communally as well as personally. Subsidiary institutions are the locus of such transformation, mustard seeds within the hostile soil of larger institutions, and live a precarious yet resilient existence. Racism needs to be understood and treated as the diminishment of being "relational self" together.[6] It is at once a religious concern and a societal ill. The good, as embodied by the recovery of dignity and equality for all people, must be maximized not only through the rejection of the evil of racism but ultimately through the transformation of evil, redirecting its energy and passion to the service of the good. This transformation is a conscious choice taken at risk with a clear sense and conviction about what is good and without an assurance of the accomplishment of its intended end. Subsidiary institutions such as families, churches, and neighborhood organizations act as agents of transformation in the face of the evil of racism. Ironically, they are also the same subsidiary institutions that most effectively perpetuate racism in the most entrenched fashion. Our confrontation with racism must recognize and move past a culture of distrust, a climate of alienation inherent in racism, to see that a new dynamic of human interaction, a new vision of human relatedness, is affirmed and respected. Paulo Freire echoes this in his assessment of oppression: "Authentic help means that all who are involved help each other mutually, growing together in the common effort to understand the reality which seeks to transform. Only through such praxis—in which those who help and those who are being helped help each other simultaneously—can the act of helping become free from the distortion in which the helper dominates the helped."[7] Our challenge is not merely a struggle against an unjust society that stifles dignity. The challenge is to move out of silence and recover speech, which permits communion with one another—breaking bread together, for which people so deeply yearn and which we Christians confess to be our deeply held value. Racism, a powerful evil force in our contemporary society, is a sign of unredeemed creation. It is real and powerful. But its reality is never permanent, nor is it ever completely separated from righteousness and justice. Hence it is capable of redemption by the process of the world spirit, the grace of God, or the redemptive activity of people even though the end of racism cannot be discernibly assured.

We need to pose the question about moral possibility in the midst of the seduction to violence and nihilism that accompanies racism. We do so not by legalism and moralism or "tortured conscience." Subversive questioning is linked to the public world, concerned with neighbor and political reality, with power and brutality, violence and fear, and the counter themes of trust, reconciliation, and waiting. It is at once religiously personal and public, not rooted in our own being but, at least for Christians, in the overriding Presence whose larger purposes can be and are served in the midst of conflicting interests and yearnings. Theologically, our discussion about racism leads us to ways of yielding to purposes that call us beyond ourselves. By squarely facing the ominous reality of racism in our midst, with its negation of the web of humanity and the absence of direction expressed through the devaluation of life in violence, we move away from romantic self-deception. By yielding to the larger purposes of the One who grants us life, we come to acknowledge a reality about ourselves that we may be inclined to deny otherwise. By so doing we are also led through that reality, accompanied by the One who moves in reality and works new purpose in life. Our discussion about racism is therefore driven by the very confessional stance we take about life, rooted in the power of our faith heritage. We must find a way through the distancing inclination toward power and violence and yearning for peace and justice, forging a new vision for human relatedness even in the midst of life's ambiguity.

"We Shall Not Be Moved"—Neighbors as the Proximate Source of Hope amid a Racist Society

Racism in our society as it impinges on communities of color and the moral possibility in the midst of violence and estrangement are amply documented. When racism is discussed by people of color, their voices often take on the character of lamentation and anguish, not a voice of resignation but a bewailing voice that yearns for an alternative life. These voices recognize and assert that evil is real and powerful. They are not dispassionate, reasoned statements about theodicy but cries of hurt and mourning. These voices are often the voices of our neighbors, who refuse to knuckle under to the powers and principalities, expressing an alternative reading of reality and life.

The lamenting voices of people of color regard racism as a powerful societal evil that makes them invisible. While rage and resentment are present in such voices, their basic tone characterizes a hope against hope born out of bewailing. These voices maintain a form of life and engage in a construction of social reality that is an alternative to the dominant social reality centered in the monopoly of imagination. The work of healing is done by communities consisting of neighbors and people of vision. By insisting that uncredentialed gatherings of neighbors are the fulcrum of rehabilitation, the anguished and bewailing voices of people of color are speeches of hope that proclaim that new life is possible. Conventional and dominant societal ideologies cast morality as a closed system in which we only "get what is coming to us" economically, politically, and socially. Against this, the voices of uncredentialed communities dare to assert that there are unadministered forces outside the dominant system that may intrude with newness and healing. Life is not reduced to an explanation or a contract. These voices dare to affirm and act on the claim that pain, anguish, and bewailing brought to speech are the powerful force to new life.

The Chicago hearings on *Racism as a Violation of Human Rights,* cosponsored by the World Council of Churches and the National Council of Churches, U.S.A., illuminate an intersection of the monopoly of imagination by the dominant culture and the subversive power of gatherings of uncredentialed people of color. The hearings are a part of the International Ecumenical Human Rights Campaign, conducted in various cities throughout the United States. Twenty witnesses—African Americans, Latinos, Asian Americans, American Indians, and Anglo-European Americans—presented nine hours of testimony on "racism as a violation of human rights." The hearings declared: "Racism limits access to educational opportunity and adequate health care, reduces the chances of economic security, and increases the odds of incarceration for young African-American and Latino males. It affects family stability, encourages drug dependency, destroys self-esteem, and promotes nihilism and despair on the part of people of color as well as ignorance and fear on the part of whites."[8] The discussion is posited, at the same time, within the Universal Declaration of Human Rights that "all human beings are born free and equal in dignity and rights." The vision of peoplehood based on the Universal Declaration undergirds imagination at the margin in the midst of the overwhelming reality of the evil of racism. The negation of relation and the absence of direction that undergird racism are reflected in the words spoken at the hearings—"incarceration," "nihilism," "despair," "ignorance," and "fear." But the Chicago hearings do not challenge merely the evil of racism. The hearings identified six areas as "critical fronts" in the struggle for racial justice: education, housing, criminal justice, employment, health care, and colonialism. These fronts point to something more than the need for a moral censorship of society. Expressed throughout the hearings are voices of a vision of what it means to be people based on the Universal Declaration of Human Rights. The challenge to racism, a transformational experience, does not take place in a sphere in which creative energy operates without contradiction, but in a sphere in which evil and good, despair and hope, incarceration and community involvement, the power of nihilism and destruction and the power of rebirth dwell side by side. The life-giving forces of the good that we encounter in life and that dwell in the life of common peoplehood do not hover above the demonic, but penetrate it, exposing the parasitical nature of racism. This is the basic theological framework in which racism is understood and challenged in the Chicago hearings.

The hearings point this out as they describe racism as "a violation of human rights" and dignity. Their description of racism is couched within the vision articulated by poet Maya Angelou, who uses the words "We shall not be moved" to express the tenacity and determination of people of color to confront racism even in the midst of circumstances of severe adversity.[9] The evil of racism, as the hearings point out, is not absolute and unredeemable. It is bound up with the very vision that is carved out of the pain of racism, voices of lament, which is "the camp of the righteous" and "the tents of the free" in such a way that both are parts of a larger process, of a greater whole, which is at once origin and goal. Thus the evil of racism is recognized as having reality, even if only that of a temporary accompaniment of unredeemed creation; but its reality is never absolute, nor is it ever completely divorced from the vision of "the camp of the righteous" and "the tents of the free." "We shall not be moved," declared the people at the hearings. These words are not a mere expression of optimism. They are words coming out of a full awareness of the evil of racism that have ripened wisdom. They are pain and anguish brought to speech in the community that takes the hard path and the narrow gate to new life.

Unmitigated Grief of Isolation as the Parlance of Hope for Relationship Rebuilding: Racism in Housing, Employment, and Health Care

A common thread identified by the Chicago hearings in regard to racism in housing, employment, and health care is the diminishing of a comprehensive sense of community and an increasing fragmentation of people based on the fear of color. The hearings noted that:

> Chicago seems to be a prime example of apartheid American style. The city is segregated by structure and by design. . . . The number of Chicago homeless now numbers over four hundred thousand [as of 1994]. Four of five are African-American, one in thirteen is Latino, and one in ten is white. . . . Inequities in health care are intimately connected with issues of employment, adequate housing and education. Communities where people are preoccupied with the business of survival—a steady paycheck, a roof, heat, and food to eat—are more likely to view health care, and especially preventative medicine, as a luxury.[10]

Racism in housing, employment, and health care is a major assault on the formation of community across racial lines, primarily because of the refusal on the part of a wider society and those who are advantaged in Chicago to see the reality of the poor, particularly the poor of color. The hearings insist that Chicago take seriously the evil of racism as an isolation (apartheid) of one person from another, one community from another, and the resulting acuteness of grief, pain, rage, and impoverishment of life for people of color in particular and society as a whole. Only with such an acknowledgment would an alternative reading of life emerge.

Until then, "we shall not be moved." As long as there is business as usual, then there is no newness, no fresh insight into an alternative way of living and understanding life. It is the public bewailing of pain and anguish that is the engine of energy for liberation. The cry of pain focuses energy and identifies truth at the margins. The dominant order is zealous to cover over the bewailing. The Chicago hearings insist that people of color shall not be moved or knuckle under in debilitating ways. The voices of those who pain and wail need to be heard because these voices are an act of truthtelling by those who refuse to acknowledge defeat even in the face of internalized and institutionalized racism.

There are a variety of theories about what is causing the problem of widespread poverty among people of color. The conservative wing of our society sees the problem of the urban poor within the welfare system. The claim is that welfare discourages people from getting jobs or getting married and encourages people to have more children and collect more welfare benefits. Remove welfare benefits, the argument goes, and people would be forced to find jobs and get married before they think about having children, therefore lessening poverty. Radical racial essentialists see the problem in the white establishment. The system that whites have created helps whites at the expense of other racial groups, causing poverty. Change the system that works against people of color, and poverty would go away. The Chicago hearings see neither of these two views as being correct. The hearings make the case that the increasing social isolation of the poor, especially the African American and Latino poor, has greatly contributed to their poverty.[11] They argue that the fundamental cause of poverty among the poor of color is segregation, or "American style apartheid." Despite all of the advances made by the civil rights movement, progress on housing desegregation has been painfully slow. The vast majority of large cities are divided geographically along racial bounds. "Out of sight, out of mind" allows the privileged people to either deny or forget the conditions in the ghetto. Ironically, we expect the poor of color to live like the privileged while at the same time cutting them off from the examples and institutions necessary for them to do so. The evil of separation and isolation (apartheid) runs amok without a clear sense of a vision of peoplehood when it comes to the matters of housing, employment, and health care. Sharing neighborhood together is critical to ordering community. Coveting counters the respect for one's neighbor and thus erodes human relationships.

William Julius Wilson's distinction between historical racism and current racism reveals the complexity of the isolation of the underclass of color. While current or "new" racism undoubtedly contributes to poverty, in Wilson's view the lingering effect of historical racism is the real culprit. African Americans, especially, have historically been relegated to low-skill jobs through discrimination in education and employment practices. With "modernization," that is, mechanization of Southern agriculture, such low-skill jobs were shifted mostly to the industrial centers of the Northeast. Now that industries are abandoning cities for suburbs and even for other countries, many African Americans are stranded in the cities and have neither job opportunities nor financial means to leave the city to go where the jobs are. The resulting unemployment has created an environment filled with crime and poverty, contributing to the breakdown of the two-parent family.

Massey and Denton echo Wilson's study, showing that segregation has created black ghettos that perpetuate the underclass by limiting the educational and employment opportunities for the residents of these neighborhoods.[12] This happens because the wealthier and white residents leave the area for the suburbs, decreasing the tax base, which hurts funding for education and other services. This in turn causes those who can afford it to leave, further decreasing the tax base and needed services. Businesses are reluctant to invest in these areas. The result is that the only people who are left are underclass people of color. They have little opportunity for education or employment, and are trapped in a vicious cycle of poverty. When the underclass of color do try to leave the ghetto, they are subjected to a variety of discrimination techniques that are designed to steer them back into their segregated neighborhoods.

Many of the civil rights battles that were won were too frequently transformed into new and more sophisticated barriers to the ever elusive equality. Both the individual opportunity programs of the 1960s and the race-based programs of the 1970s and 1980s had a disproportionate effect on upper- and middle-class people of color. Contrary to popular belief, segregation is not at its worst in the South, but in the North. In 1966, Martin Luther King came to Chicago and declared it "the most segregated city in America." Despite King's and all the other civil rights leaders' efforts, little has changed. Chicago is only 5 percent more integrated today than it was in 1970, and it retains the title of America's most segregated city.

Before the turn of the century, however, blacks and whites were quite integrated. The mass migration of Southern blacks to the cities in the North in the first two decades of the century coincided with mass influxes of immigrants. The new arrivals lived separately in their own neighborhoods. After the Great Depression and World War II, government housing policies favored whites at the expense of those in the African American neighborhoods, causing a white flight to the suburbs, leaving African Americans isolated in the ghettos of the inner city. The early civil rights movement focused on removing barriers to equal participation and competition by African Americans. But, as Wilson points out, inequalities remain after bias is diminished. While desegregation allowed African Americans to move into white suburbs, only relatively wealthy African Americans could actually afford a house there. Race-based programs like affirmative action aimed at remedying past injustices are also often only relevant to wealthier people of color. As we see later in the section on racism in education, poor blacks are less likely to apply for college, so they do not directly benefit from equal opportunity in higher education. Civil rights programs, contrary to their purpose, sometimes exacerbated poor blacks' problems by providing avenues of escape for better-off African Americans. As indicated earlier, urban black communities were left without this class of "social buffers," who comprised the main support for institutions like churches and schools and who provided role models for poor and wealthy African American children alike. A clear sense of peoplehood is absent in such a situation. Today, poor black children are less likely to know two-parent families or people who have steady work. The link between hard work and success is missing. As Cornel West points out, without these buffers poor children are left at the mercy of a consumption-oriented society. Movies and television are quick to show the glamour of the rich, but they fail to show the hard work that accompanies such a status achievement.

The Chicago hearing suggests that what is disturbing is the possibility that we live in a society in which racism has become so institutionalized and internalized that it is a major driving force for the maintenance of the existing societal system. Apartheid American style is the monopoly of imagination that keeps our whole society in bondage to its powers and principalities in this sense. An honest acknowledgment of this reality and its deep pain for those who are victimized by it is a necessary prerequisite to the emergence of an alternative vision of life. Denial and refusal to see reality as it truly is are major obstacles to eradicating the societal evil of racism.

The main problem identified in *Racism in Health Care* is the establishment of a variety of barriers to health care, endangering the health and well-being of underprivileged people of color but also contributing to the deepening gulf of separation and fragmentation among all those who constitute society. The Chicago hearings point out that "inequities in health care are intimately connected with issues of employment, adequate housing and education. Communities where people are preoccupied with the business of survival—a steady paycheck, a roof, heat, and food to eat are more likely to view health care, and especially preventative medicine, as a luxury." There is a close link between racism in housing and employment and racism in health care. For people of color, particularly for those who are socioeconomically disadvantaged, race is the major reason the United States has a health care system that is plagued with disparities. The racial conflict in the United States from preindustrial through modern times has created and exacerbated disparities in the quality of health care.

Howard E. Freeman's study reveals these disparities: There has been a deterioration in the already limited access to medical care for the nation's poor, uninsured, and a significant segment of people of color.[13] The study reports four findings with regard to the access to care people of color receive: (1) Americans' overall use of medical care has declined in terms of visits to physicians; (2) access to physician care for the economically disadvantaged and uninsured decreased between 1982 and 1986; (3) people of color receive less hospital care than whites who suffer from the same illnesses; and (4) a significant number of people of color underutilize important health services. Although the article was published in 1987, the same problems continue to haunt the health care system in the United States today. Ten years have passed and this nation is still in the same (if not a worse) position as it was ten years ago with regard to the issue of people of color's access to health care.

Sidney Watson's study on health care in the inner city underscores this reality.[14] He begins with a story of a pregnant woman of color who had no insurance, no money, and no prenatal care, and whom the local private hospital did not want to admit. With this story Watson introduces the reality that health care for the poor is neither equal nor quality. Watson states that the poverty rate for African American families is three times the rate for white families. Only about half of all African Americans have private health insurance; one in five has Medicaid or Medicare; and one in five has no health coverage. The article demonstrates that African Americans—particularly poor, inner-city African Americans—have greater health care needs than whites. Although African American inner-city residents have many illnesses and need more medical care than other Americans, they have less access to health care. Federal budget cuts have forced many inner-city primary care clinics to close, and private hospitals have abandoned the inner city. The facilities that closed served twice as many African American patients and twice as many Medicaid patients as the hospitals that remained open. The private hospitals that remained behind often limited the number of Medicaid patients treated, disproportionately excluding African American patients who, as stated earlier, are five times as likely as whites to be covered by Medicaid.

Vernellia R. Randall extensively examined how racism in America establishes separate and independent barriers to health care institutions and to medical care.[15] He, too, emphasizes the importance of understanding the full extent of differences in health care between African Americans and European Americans as essential to fully appreciating the need for reform in the health care system and to understanding the inadequacies in current reform approaches that do not recognize these differences. Without the health care system affording African Americans an opportunity to enjoy decent health, Randall asserts that it is virtually impossible for African Americans to gain other resources, such as money and an education, which are necessary to gain success in the American economic system. Therefore, "when African Americans are sick and poor, they are just as enslaved as if the law made them so." Racial barriers to access can be divided into three major groups: barriers to hospitals, barriers to nursing homes, and barriers to physicians and other providers. Randall's basic premise is that in order to improve the health of African Americans, it is not sufficient merely to remove barriers to access based on socioeconomic status. Randall concludes that in order to establish a successful health care reform plan, the plan needs to provide African Americans access to the health care they need, focusing on the needs of the African American population, which differ from the needs of European Americans.

The Chicago hearings suggest that health care reformers need to address the larger question of how to improve American health generally and, specifically, the health of people of color in the inner city. This would require: (1) securing health care financing, (2) attracting sufficient health care providers into the inner city, (3) combating discrimination in the delivery of health care, and

(4) developing new health care delivery systems responsive to the needs of inner-city residents. In other words, health care institutions need to confront institutional racism. Furthermore, the hearings emphasize that certain provisions must be included in the reform package for improvements to occur, including universal coverage for all residents, comprehensive coverage of preventive and primary health care, no serious financial barriers to participation, and provider reimbursement rates for any public system comparable to those of private insurance. The Chicago hearings go on to identify and discuss methods of attracting providers as well as to discuss the likelihood that civil rights efforts can put an end to discrimination against inner-city African Americans and other people of color. Increasing access to health care by itself, however, will not improve the health of inner-city African Americans and other people of color. Socioeconomic strategies such as increased access to jobs, better schools, good housing, less crime, and more affordable transportation and food need to be implemented to ensure that the health of poor inner-city people of color is improved.

Traditional solutions to societal problems have failed because victims of societal inequities are targeted instead of the structures that cause the problems. A sense of what constitutes well-being for society as a whole, a sense of peoplehood, must be developed. Many existing programs reinforce the idea that poverty is unavoidable and people should accept this proposition, while the heart of the problem in health care for people of color is the same as in the case of housing and employment: "Apartheid, American style." Indeed, the description of health care concerns in Apartheid South Africa given by Elena Nightingale echoes the very issues of health care in the United States:

Apartheid remains a prime cause of the unequal and racially discriminatory provision of funds for health services; of the over-crowding of the ill-equipped black hospitals and the underutilization of white hospitals; of miserable housing, gross pollution, poor sanitation, and lack of health care. . . . Apartheid, in consequence, is the underlying structure causing the dreadful burden of excess morbidity and mortality, much of it preventable, that is borne by the black population. These health-specific effects are superimposed on the more general consequences of Apartheid which bars the majority of South African citizens from participating in decisions on the allocation of resources for health or other needs.[16]

The health care system is fundamentally flawed under such a circumstance, Nightingale concludes. For a large segment of the population of color, the whole spectrum of health services, but most urgently primary care, is inadequate. As a result, entire generations suffer through much of their lifetimes. The effects of the current state of health care persist for generations, in part because of the health consequences of the profound poverty that racism itself has engendered and in part because widespread attitudes that encourage racism, elitism, and prejudice against the poor, particularly of color, take time and commitment to change. Racism and discrimination have made this society a symbol of human rights violations in the area of health care and services.

Isolation is the primary cause of poverty for people of color. What is needed, the Chicago hearings point out, is to provide the poor of all races with the resources necessary to compete for jobs, or what William Julius Wilson calls "equality of life chances." Perhaps one way of meeting such a challenge is to create a national strategy to make the workforce more adaptable to change, such as the creation of more jobs as part of a federal macroeconomic policy that strives for a tight labor market and noninflationary economic growth. What is called for is the means to create universal benefits such as child care and medical care, which would level the playing field so that everyone would have equal resources to compete. Also called for is the formation of community ties, which would promote mobility of the poor. While getting money to the poor is important, so is ending their isolation. Are these suggestions idealistic and unrealistic dreams to be attained? Perhaps, if the real issue of racism is its internalized and institutionalized powers and principalities. "We shall not be moved" is the basic posture of the Chicago hearings, a speech of defiance that is expressed out of the pain of segregation and isolation. The only real source of hope lies in the efforts of caring neighbors. The Chicago hearings identified such subsidiary organizations as Habitat for Humanity, which go into the ghetto, getting to know the poor as individuals rather than as "the poor." Actually knowing people in the ghetto can mean the formation of community ties and feelings of mutual responsibility. An urban peace corps such as President Clinton has proposed might be a step in the right direction. The hearings saw the formation of a commonly shared neighborhood community as the expression of defiance for our fragmenting and racist society.

A fundamental assault on the well-being of peoplehood takes place in a society when its wealth is measured in commodities and put away for some to have and some not to have, when a sense of solidarity yields to Darwinistic individuality, when a sense of belonging with and to each other is replaced by the drive to separation. Those who can pay and know are those who belong. They can talk only to one another and trust only one another. And so the others—the ones who cannot pay and don't know and don't belong—are left to their own resourcelessness. When financial resources, knowledge, and access are no longer shared among us all but are controlled by some, the natural network of caring community collapses. Housing, employment, and health care are no longer dependent on natural interaction among neighbors. Racism in housing, employment, and health care is not primarily a political or economic problem; it has to do with a crisis of human relations. It requires us to reflect on our assumed understanding of peoplehood coupled with the economic, technological, and intellectual elitism with which we perceive the reality of human life. Surely we have fallen into that perception without ever deciding to. And we are beset by a fearful racial tribalism that fuels the seemingly insoluble crisis of housing, employment, and health care for people of color.

The Chicago hearings, on the other hand, perceive matters of housing, employment, and health care within the context of the Universal Declaration of Human Rights—"All human beings are born free and equal in dignity and rights," including rights to housing, employment, and health care. The Declaration counters the perception of life that assumes that housing, employment, and health care belong to the privileged, to those who can pay. Privileges for some are transformed into rights for all. The capricious possession of some now becomes a gift shared by all the community for all the community. The Chicago hearings recognize a tension between these two principles. Propelled by the vision of the Declaration, with the determination that "we shall not be moved" by the principle of commodities and privileged life, racism in housing, employment, and health care is challenged with an alternative perception of peoplehood, a network of persons and neighbors in covenant with one another, who have made solemn promises of sustaining and caring, defending and enhancing one another through subsidiary agencies and communities.

Covenanting as a public act applies to the civil as well as religious communities. Peoplehood is enhanced when all community members are seriously committed to the well-being of all. Conversely, peoplehood is diminished when some members hold out on others, set themselves above others, or do not care. The transformation of the evil of racism moves from diminishment to enhancement for both individuals and peoplehood. Housing, employment, and health care are not just programs, though they are programmatic issues. Ultimately, they afford a way of perceiving the world, an affirmation about dignity, worth, and hope, a way of keeping matters in perspective so that we are not overwhelmed by our own propriety, property, knowledge, competence, or merit. When we free ourselves from coveting, the power to interact in healing ways surprises us. That is the promise we have in Christian faith.[17] An appropriate expression of such a conviction is the voice that says, "I shall not be moved," a defiant voice that we raise together amidst the full knowledge

of both the power of racism and the willingness of the racist
society to use that power.

Devaluation of Color: Racism as Colonialism and Racism in Education

To conform to the monopoly of imagination means to exact revenge
against those who depart from the norm. The inclination toward
revenge is so powerful that those who guard, honor, and benefit
from the norm become more and more exclusive. Racism in
housing, employment, and health care is the manifestation of such
an inclination. This is also the nature of racism expressed force-
fully in what is termed "domestic colonialism" and in education.
The Chicago hearings state this dynamic of conformity and exclusion: "Colonialism involves not only the political subjugation, but
more importantly, the mental and cultural subjugation of people."
The testimony on education outlined a lack of sensitivity by the
schools to the needs and desires of communities of color. "Racism,
intolerance, and indifference seem to be matters of course in the
daily lives of students and their parents. Lack of adequate minority representation in the teaching staff makes the situation critical.
Only 3–5 percent of faculty at this nation's colleges and universities are persons of color."[18] Because the dominant values are
predictably the values of the dominant class, those who have these
monopolies also come to have a monopoly of legitimacy and virtue,
land and property, and in the end a monopoly of imagination. They
control not only every benefit in the present but every imaginable
prospect for the future. The monopoly is not just a monopoly of
power but has come to be a monopoly of society's norms.

Domestic Colonialism

At the Chicago hearings the subject of domestic colonialism
and domination produced words of caution about the crucial

difference between colonized Americans and ethnic immigrants of color. African Americans are particularly aware of the danger of equating race concerns with multicultural matters. Immigrants have been able to operate relatively competitively within our society because they came voluntarily in search of a better life, because their movements in society are not administratively controlled, and because they transformed their culture at their own pace—giving up ethnic and cultural values and institutions when it was seen as a desirable exchange for improvements in social position and stable life situations. But domestic colonialization is a form of unequal institutionalized contract and resembles a master-servant, paternalistic relationship that affects those who had no choice in deciding to come to this continent. This colonization has several discernable components. The racial group's forced, involuntary entry into the country is one component. African American slaves were in this group. The impact of this interaction is much more dramatic than the slower and perhaps more natural processes of acculturation. The colonizing power carries out a policy that constrains, transforms, or even destroys indigenous values, orientations, and ways of life such as those of indigenous peoples.

Moreover, colonization involves a relationship by which members of the colonized group tend to be administered by representatives of the dominant power. There is the experience of being managed and manipulated by those who are in the position of power in terms of racial status. Then there is a comparative valuation between the dominant group and the colonized. Since one group is seen as inferior, it is exploited, controlled, and oppressed by the dominant group. It is also important to note that the initial contact of the groups was between "inferior" and "superior." Being colonized, as Michelle Cliff suggests, is being rendered insensitive, having those parts necessary for survival numbed.[19] It is abdicating responsibility for one's own self, giving over all the descriptive power of identity to someone else, blurring the edge between refusing to show one's self to hostile others and losing touch with the real because of the strain of enacting. It is the bankruptcy of personhood.

A significant effect of domestic colonialism is to weaken the will of the colonized in resisting oppression. It has been easier to contain and control the colonized because communal bonds and group solidarity are normally weakened through divisions among leadership, failures of organization, and the general dispirited-ness that accompany social oppression. As African American participants noted at the Chicago hearings, the cultures of over-seas colonies were not destroyed nearly to the extent that the African cultures of the slaves were in the United States. The language, religion, and family structures of these Africans were almost totally obliterated when they were brought into this country. Domestic colonialism in this regard is an extreme expression of the monopoly of imagination.

Racism directed to the immigration of people of color is dis-tinct from domestic colonialism, but is nonetheless another expression of the monopoly of imagination imposed on those who are vulnerable. The immigration policies of the United States reveal the underlying worldview of what constitutes peo-plehood in the United States. The Chicago hearings quote President Theodore Roosevelt:

> If the immigrant who comes here in good faith becomes an American and assimilates himself to us he shall be treated on an exact equality with everyone else . . . but this [equality] is predicated on the man's becoming in very fact an American and nothing but an American. There can be no divided allegiance here. Any who says he is an American but something else also, isn't an American at all. . . . We have room for but one language and that is the English language, for we want to see that the crucible turns our people out as Americans, of American nationality, and not as dwellers in a polyglot boarding house.[20]

The vision of peoplehood in Manifest Destiny is "assimilated Americans." However, the reality of assimilation is complex in the context of race relations. Recent discussions on colonialism have produced a binary division of assimilation versus essential-ism. The essentializing notion of "identity politics" has sometimes been criticized by scholars of color in favor of "heterogeneity, multiplicity, and nonequivalence." Another distinction is "nation-alism" versus "assimilation," in which nationalism seems reduced to a species of "fanatical nativism." There is an inherent danger in the perspective of a binary world—between the politics of an overarching and repressive identity and the self-defeating strate-gies of "difference" that lead to more and more painful fragmen-tation. What is needed is a carefully nuanced historical reading of the predicament of ethnicity.[21]

A temptation on the part of underrepresented people of color is to respond "to their experience of racial discrimination by accept-ing the racialism it presupposed."[22] Such a posture on the part of an oppressed group is bound to reproduce the evils of which it is the victim. This society needs to accept the primacy of historical specificity and the need for rich and complex negotiation with the ingredients of representation, power, and multiple spaces. We need to acknowledge that the power of assimilationist culture is not as monolithic as it seems. Immigrants come to the United States of their own accord. Some immigrants experience life in the United States as an extension of the colonialism they inher-ited in their homelands. The two ways of reading immigration—as assimilationism and as nationalism—simply obscure the complexity of the reality of immigration in the United States.

A case in point is the place of Filipino Americans in their rela-tion to both what are termed "Asian Americans" and a wider American common culture. Recent scholarship in ethnic studies sees Filipino Americans and their practice of cultural formation as no longer subsumed under the rubric of "Asian American."[23] The reason is that the Filipino Americans' homeland was originally a sovereign territory until the late sixteenth century. The attempt at independence made by Aguinaldo and others during the Spanish-American War (1898) was unsuccessful, and Spain ceded the islands to the United States in 1898. So the Filipinos traded one colonial master for another, and didn't become independent until after World War II. From 1898 to 1946, Filipinos in the United States thus were not immigrants in the conventional sense but colonial subjects whose bodies were exiled from an already peripheral existence in the Philippines to marginalized existence within the United States.[24] Their cultures were classified by the colonial group in order to legitimate its monopoly of knowledge, power, and imagination.

Filipino Americans today make up one of the largest components of the Asian American category, and they are perhaps one of the most marginalized and most misrecognized ethnic and racial constituencies in North America. Historical specificities of Filipino incorporation into the American racial formation distinguish the Filipino diaspora from its Chinese, Japanese, or Korean counterparts. Armed resistance in the Philippines to United States colonial rule and persisting oppositional nationalism have functioned as an undergirding experience motivating Filipino initiatives in labor organizing and cultural practices even in the United States. Filipinos as an oppressed nationality cannot just be lumped under the ethnic rubric of "Asian American." Furthermore, Bruce Occena and his associates argue that not only are Filipinos distinguished from other Asians by their collective experience of U.S. imperial oppression at home, but each wave of Filipino migration manifests distinctive characteristics rooted in unequal relations of power between the Philippines and the United States.[25] Occena comments: "Taken as a group, Filipinos have been integrated into U.S. society on the basis of inequality and subjected to discrimination due both to their race and nationality."[26] The misunderstanding of Filipino Americans is based on years of fallacious conventional assimilationist narratives. For the discussion of racism experienced by immigrants of color, a distinction of historical contexts of immigration is necessary. Nevertheless, regardless of these important distinctions, colonialism is the primary cultural structure by which racism manifests itself for Filipino and other immigrants of color.

By implication, the paradigm of ethnic assimilation to this society and its normative code becomes the measure of group legitimacy and success for colonized people of color. In the midst of the forces of assimilation, racialized subordination of certain immigrants of color such as the Filipinos in the United States has produced cultures of resistance that have accompanied the process of forced incorporation or assimilation. However, the culture of resistance by and large did not result in the formation of a militant and exclusive nationalistic group or a reactionary group of cultural insulation. Rather, the culture of resistance takes on a translocal character, encompassing the cultural and ethnic distinctness of a group while at the same time bridging ethnic American communities and communities abroad. In this case, the "neighbors" are those who live across an ocean. The subsidiary community is stretched across a wide distance. Nevertheless, it is still a community where life is coherent and supportive, and it serves as the source of dignity. The message is that of determined existence and the claim for legitimation according to their own norms and expectations even as they negotiate with persistent assimilationist forces. Filipino American communities and many Latino and Hispanic communities are creating such an emerging pattern in response to the devaluation of their communities in racialized colonialism.

Racial Vulnerability in Education

Learning is indeed the meeting of minds that leads to the discovery of human initiative, capacity, courage, and limitation. Learning is the exploration of what we are able to do, what we are expected to do, and what we are permitted to do. Learning challenges those who in their high valuation of their own competence are possessed by their possessions. Learning in this sense points to liberation. Learning reminds those who have given up on life of the power of life. Learning imparts hope amidst the twin threats of cynicism and despair. Learning nurtures and cultivates community through the cultivation of mutual respect, care, and values. In the segment called *Racism in Education,* the

Chicago hearings point to the disturbing impact of the devaluing of people of color and the creation of racial vulnerability in Chicago's educational system. Even the term "racism" risks missing the full scope of racial devaluation in our society, implying as it does that racial devaluation comes primarily from those who are strongly prejudiced, not from just any person. But the existence of "racists," deplorable though racism is, misses the full extent of the burden that devalued persons carry. This burden becomes acute in education.

Devaluation grows out of our images of society and the way those images catalog people. The catalog need not be taught. It is implied by all we see around us: the kinds of people worshiped in advertising and movies, conversations about whether a person of color can be President, and who is noteworthy enough to be included in school curricula and literary and musical canons. The ways people are valued and respected create an image of society in which many Americans of color simply do not fare well. A saying among grade school children captures the reality: "If you're white you're right, if you're yellow you're mellow, if you're brown stick around, but if you're black get back." These images reinforce the standards against which information about people of color is evaluated. These images also set up a double jeopardy of devaluation for people of color, a jeopardy that does not necessarily apply to people belonging to the racially dominant group.

People of color have the extra fear that in the eyes of those around them their full humanity could fall with the mispronunciation of words, a poor answer, or a misspelling. The risk is that such "failures" will confirm the broader racial inferiority they are suspected of. This fear manifests itself, for example, among Asian Americans in the form of being a "model minority," an attempt to emulate the dominant intellectual culture and excel according to its standards.

Moreover, because these images are conditioned in all of us and collectively held, they can spawn racial devaluation in all of us, not just in the strongly prejudiced. They can do this even in people of color themselves: children of color, for example, preferring to play with white dolls rather than dolls of color. Thus people of color and their own self-devaluation can come from a circle of people far greater than the expressly prejudiced, which circle includes teachers, mentors, and perhaps even parents. Tragically, such devaluation can seem inescapable. Sooner or later it forces on its victims painful realizations. One such realization is that society is preconditioned to see the worst in them. Students of color quickly learn that acceptance, if it is to be won at all, will be hard-won. Another is that even if a student of color gains approval in one setting, such an approval will have to be won again at the next level of schooling. Thus, students of color are left deeply vulnerable in America's classrooms. A high dropout rate among people of color reflects this reality.

Thus the racial devaluation of people of color that is so prevalent in society breeds conformity to the prevailing monopoly of imagination in education. Forced conformity to the dominant norms and values of our society excludes those who depart from those norms. Children come to school with racism already imparted by parents, peers, the media, and the various socializing agencies in the community, or what educator Melvin Tumin of Princeton calls "the transmission belts of prejudice."[27] Thus the wall of separation and isolation based on hostility becomes reinforced in the educational system. The Chicago hearings describe this reality: "Racism, intolerance, and indifference seem to be matters of course in the daily lives of students and their parents. Lack of adequate minority representation in teaching staff makes the situation critical. . . . The crisis of confidence in Chicago Public Schools' ability to educate young people of color was seriously called into question."[28] Exclusion of those who are "different" through the monopolizing power of the dominant group's imagination undergirds racial devaluation in education, subverting the formation of a peoplehood based on mutual respect, hospitality, and trust.

The Chicago hearings point out the complex structural dynamics of racial exclusion through devaluation operating in education. For example, the dropout rate for minority youth under the age of sixteen is 50 percent in the Chicago public schools. There is a significant lack of adequate representation of people of color in teaching staff. Racial resegregation of schools is an emerging pattern in Chicago. This is done by the privatization of schools, "white flight" to the suburbs, and the inequities of state funding for schools. There is also a correlation between inadequate education and lack of employment opportunities: students who drop out or who have negative experiences in school are much more likely to have difficulties in finding employment, since they have not developed the skills necessary for successful competition. Given these and other factors involved in the systemic nature of racism in education, the hearings named the central issue as the "intolerance and indifference" that continue to be perpetuated in the lives of students, teachers, and parents. In other words, central to racism in education is the disintegration of the web of relationship that makes up citizenry through a pattern of exclusion and racial devaluation. Racism in education undermines the foundational underpinning of what it means to be people and to build community.

Since the sixties, when race relations were seen with an optimistic yearning for a new age, the persistence of racism with its new manifestations has resulted in "problem fatigue"—resignation to an unwanted condition of life. This fatigue deadens our senses to the deepening crisis in the education of people of color. One can enter any desegregated school in America, from grade school to high school to graduate or professional school, and meet a persistent reality: African Americans and Hispanic Americans on the one hand and whites on the other live in largely separate worlds. Asian Americans are seen as a "model minority" whose achievements and abilities are measured by the dominant cultural and intellectual standards. The perception that has emerged is that these worlds are not equal, either in the education taking place there or in the achievement of the students who occupy them.

What really undermines the achievement of people of color is "stigma," the endemic devaluing of people of color in our society and schools. This stigma creates its own condition of life, different from class, money, or culture. This stigma is capable of "breaking the claim" that one's human attributes have on people.[29] The relationship between such a stigma and schooling is a part of race relations that has been vastly underappreciated and continues to fester in our society. On the other hand, this reading points to another fact: If people of color are made less racially vulnerable in school, they can overcome even substantial obstacles. This is the alternative understanding of life from which the issues of education for people of color need to be discussed. But in the meantime, the worsening crisis in education continues for a large number of students of color. Despite their socioeconomic disadvantages as a group, people of color in general begin school with test scores that are fairly close to the test scores of whites their age. The longer they stay in school, however, the more they fall behind. This pattern exists in even the most elite American colleges. Tragically, low grades can render a degree essentially "terminal" in the sense that they preclude further schooling.

A familiar set of explanations is given. One is societal disadvantage. It is true that people of color have had and continue to have more than their share: a history of slavery, segregation, and job ceilings; continued lack of economic opportunity; poor schools; and the related problems of broken families, drug-infested communities, and social isolation. Any of these factors, singly or combined, can undermine school achievement. But the achievement deficits appear to occur even when students of color suffer no major financial disadvantage—among middle-class students on wealthy college campuses and in graduate school among those students receiving substantial financial aid. Another myth needs to be countered: Even economically disadvantaged people of color value education highly, often more than those who are of the dominant racial group. Several programs have improved African American school achievement without addressing culturally specific learning orientations or doing anything to remedy socioeconomic disadvantage. Neither is the problem fully explained by deficits in skill or preparation that people of color might suffer because of background disadvantages.[30] Dinesh D'Souza has argued recently that college affirmative-action programs cause failure and high dropout rates among African American students by recruiting them to levels of college work for which they are inadequately prepared. That was clearly not the case.

Furthermore, something depresses the achievement of many students of color from grade school to graduate school (with perhaps the exception of Asian Americans) at every level of preparation. It is true that the better prepared achieve better than the less prepared, and this is about as true for people of color as for whites. But given any level of school preparation, people of color somehow achieve less in subsequent schooling than whites no matter how strong that preparation is. The same achievement level requires better preparation for people of color than for whites. This is a racial tragedy.

While social and economic advantages certainly contribute, students of color tend to underachieve even when they have ample resources, strongly value education, and are prepared better than adequately in terms of knowledge and skills. The reason is that the primary contributing factor for underachievement is the lack of schooling that provides a climate for nurturing self-esteem. The root of the achievement problems for a large majority of people of color is the failure of schooling to meet this simple condition for many of its students. Doing well in school requires a belief that school achievement can be a promising basis of self-esteem and self-affirmation. That belief needs constant reaffirmation even for advantaged students. Tragically, many students of color are still haunted by a specter that threatens this belief and the identification that derives from it at every level of schooling. In significant part the crisis in American education stems from the absence of an educational climate for nurturing self-esteem and respect.

Racial devaluation is based on the dialectic of conformity and exclusion, just as in the case of colonialism and racism. The basic assimilationist offer that schools make to people of color is this: You can be valued and rewarded in school (and society) but you as a student must first master the culture and ways of the

American mainstream. Since that mainstream (as it is represented) is essentially white, this means the student must give up
many particulars of being a person of color—styles of speech and
appearance, value priorities, preferences—at least in mainstream
settings. These subtle and yet pervasive expectations contribute
to the diminishing of self-esteem for people of color. They have
been the "color-blind" offer to every immigrant and minority
group in our nation's history, the core of the melting-pot ideal.

Some people of color accept these expectations and excel in
meeting them. Yet nonimmigrants such as African Americans
and Native Americans have always been here, and thus are enti-
tled, more than new immigrants, to participate in the defining
images of society projected in school. More important, their
exclusion from these images denies their contributive history
and presence in society. Thus, whereas immigrants can tilt
toward assimilation in pursuit of the opportunities for which
they came, African Americans may find it harder to assimilate.
For them, the offer of acceptance in return for assimilation carries a primal insult: it asks them to join in something that has
made them invisible. This is the issue that distinguishes African
Americans and Native Americans from other people of color.

And yet, there is a common thread that affects all people of
color. Deep in the psyche of American education is a presumption that students of color need academic remediation to overcome background deficits. This orientation guides many efforts
to close the achievement gap. But for too many students of
color, school is the place where, more persistently and authori-
tatively than anywhere else in society, they learn how little they
are valued and respected. The monopoly of imagination leads to
the heart of racism in education, stigmatizing the very being of
people of color, making difficult the possibility of relational
rebuilding across racial lines.

The challenge is therefore in valuing people of color for who
and what they are. The challenge is how to speak with seriousness of the reality of devaluation and the buoyancy of overriding
claims that can preempt the evil of racism. Holding together the

seriousness and the buoyancy cannot be done only through following the narrative of the dominant community as it chooses.
Such is the nature of hope, the resilient conviction that the
processes of human interaction are to be understood in relation
to some overriding purpose that prevails in odd but uncompro-
mising ways. Erving Goffman uses the term "wise" to describe
people who do not themselves bear the stigma of a given group
but who are accepted by the group.[31] These are people in whose
eyes the full humanity of the stigmatized is visible, people in
whose eyes they feel less vulnerable. If racial vulnerability undermines school achievement of people of color, then this achievement should improve significantly if schooling is made "wise"—
that is, made to see value and promise in students of color and to
act accordingly. The primary purpose of education, then, is to
instill the message that one is valued because of one's academic
potential regardless of the current skill level of the student.

Vision Breaks Through Brokenness in the Numbed Culture of the Criminal Justice System

Nowhere is the collapse of peoplehood so starkly revealed and
the violent hand of racism forced upon people of color as in the
arena of criminal justice. All else follows the imagination about
life captured in the assumptions we bring to criminal justice.
Paul Ricoeur's words speak to this reality: "And it is in the heart
of our imagination that we let the Event happen, before we may
convert our heart and tighten our will."[32] Racism, the pathology
of our time, is the reduction of imagination so that we become
too numbed, satiated, and co-opted to do serious reflective and
imaginative work. Our current criminal justice system reveals
our enslavement to the monopoly of imagination from which our
society is incapable of being freed. It could be that those who
are incarcerated within the system can imagine and articulate
something different, an alternative vision of life. And yet they
have a hard time finding a place and a way for their voices.

"The criminal justice system is one area where racism is often the most pronounced and the most tragic. Desperation about issues like joblessness, homelessness, and lack of economic opportunity can lead to involvement in drugs, prostitution, and gangs. These paths often lead to a direct confrontation with law enforcement and the criminal justice system—a system historically set up to protect the property, health and well-being of those who hold political power." These are the findings of the Chicago hearings. The hearings call for a comprehensive, provocative examination of the embattled crossroads at which race relations in America intersect with the criminal justice system. Racism in one of its most violent forms is seen in today's criminal justice system. It is the perception of life, an imagination, based on the notion of elimination of the unwanted, undesirable, and failed from our midst. The criminal justice system as we have it is a blatant expression of the collapse of peoplehood. Randall Kennedy in his work *Race, Crime, and the Law* talks about the need for reorienting our thinking about race and criminal justice: "This effort to reorient thinking about the race question in criminal law is animated by a sense that inherited debates between liberals and conservatives have become increasingly sterile. It is also animated by a belief that useful prescriptions for problems as complex as those generated by the imperatives of law enforcement in our large, rambunctious, multiracial society can arise only from thinking that frees itself of reflexive obedience to familiar signals." Kennedy sees the monopoly of imagination in the current criminal justice system: "Attuned to the reported demographics of crime, fearful people of all hues engage in race-dependent strategies either to apprehend criminals or to avoid them." A counter imagination to the "familiar signals" of this prevailing imagination of our society is "to facilitate the emergence of a policy that is overwhelmingly indifferent to racial differences, a policy that looks beyond looks."[33] Where do we find voices that speak to such a policy, voices of those who are not enslaved by the dominant value assumptions about criminal justice?

Our society is vitally concerned about crime. Since the early 1980s we have been assaulted by images of devastated neighborhoods and destitute families, of urban gangs running amok and besieged police officers either pummeling or being pummeled by an ever bolder criminal element. In reaction to our understandable concern, our politicians most often have dealt with the problem of crime in America by "getting tough," by stiffening sentences, expanding police forces, and building prisons. A conventional reading is to see criminals as simply social misfits who resist the civilizing effects of American culture. A more accurate reading is that American culture itself produces the conditions in which crime and violence flourish. In other words, there is a political agenda at work here, one designed to shift attention away from the failings of our economic system and scapegoat a certain segment of people of color in the process.

The law-and-order agenda of campaigning politicians continues to shape the perception that crime, particularly violent crime, is spiraling out of control. As a result, while other areas of government spending are cut back, criminal justice continues to be a burgeoning industry. In fact, the "crime control" industry has exploded in state and local governments today, and these governments spend more on the criminal justice system than on education. The reality is that statistics suggest that crime rates, particularly rates of violent crime, are dropping. In most large cities in the United States, crime has decreased for the fourth consecutive year. However, the public is continually barraged by media reports of horrific crimes. Embedded in the hysteria surrounding the alleged rise in crime is a racism that criminalizes poor people and particularly people of color. Criminals as defined by the current criminal justice system have been cast as a class of people predisposed to violent activities. Kennedy points out "the disability of being perceived as people wholly devoid of moral choice and thus blameless for purposes of retribution, the same way that infants, the insane and animals are typically viewed as morally blameless." Categorizing groups of people becomes a substitute for genuinely addressing the ills of society, reducing the issues of criminal justice to punitive measures rather than prevention.

President Clinton's Omnibus Crime Bill, passed in August 1994, institutionalizes a perspective that focuses on catching criminals rather than preventing crime, including hiring 100,000 new police officers and spending $10 billion for the construction of new federal prisons. The "three strikes" proposal mandates life sentences for anyone convicted of three "violent" felonies (or even "attempts" to commit such felonies) or of two "violent" offenses and one "serious" drug felony. It also allows children as young as thirteen to be tried as adults. The United States already jails a larger proportion of its people than any other country in the world.

The reality is that none of these moves is really about curtailing crime. Research shows that the police are extremely ineffective when it comes to crime prevention. Furthermore, as the American Bar Association's Task Force on Crime has noted, "there is no solid evidence to support the conclusion that sending more convicted offenders to prison for longer periods of time deters others from committing crime." The traditional solutions are also the cornerstones of a racist criminal justice system. Incarceration rates, rates for persons on death row, rates for those involved in other parts of the criminal justice system—all these statistics testify to the differential impact the criminal justice system has on economically marginalized people. In 1991 in the United States, African American males between the ages of fifteen and thirty-four made up 14 percent of the population and more than 40 percent of those in prison. In Washington, D.C., and Baltimore, 40 to 50 percent of all black men between the ages of eighteen and thirty-five are either in prison, in jail, on probation or parole, or under warrant for arrest.[34] Who are these crime-prone males and what makes them crime-prone? The general perception is that they are poor and invisible people of color (and the two often go hand-in-hand) confined to the inner city. The law-and-order agenda thus has the ideological purpose of distracting public attention from substantive issues such as poverty and unemployment. A conventional response to the problems of poverty relies heavily on the notion of "taking responsibility for your actions." By effectively criminalizing those who perpetrate crimes, people's basic needs are sidetracked. Criminals are seen as a class of people to be suppressed, tricked, and hunted down. If criminals are characterized as people of color, poor, or young, then a significant proportion of the class that struggles with the failures of the economic system can be repressed by the criminal justice system.[35] Also, by constructing a picture of who is most likely to be a criminal, those who use the rhetoric create stereotypes that they can use in their fear mongering.

Scapegoating by the criminal justice system also feeds anti-immigration attitudes and policies and deflects people's attention from the failures they are experiencing in the system. For all these reasons, the law-and-order panic needs to be seen for what it is: a means of perpetuating racism that provides an ideological cover for the failures of the system, supports the maintenance of the ruling class, and functions as a tool of social control that divides working-class people.

Once again in the criminal justice system we find a crisis of value categories and discernment. Our practice of criminal justice makes us ask if we really want the perceptions in which life is a set of problems to be solved, manageable possibilities are all that are considered, and those who have failed in society are to be put away and eliminated. Behind this utilitarian discernment of life lies a connection between concentration of power and wealth and violence. It is the thirst to kill in order to control. We are always close to blood, either as perpetrator or as victim, in both cases overwhelmed by a violence we can neither justify or deny and that goes mostly unacknowledged. The Chicago hearings pose the question about moral possibility in the midst of all our seduction to violence and vengeance.

In a collection of fiercely poignant essays, a prison inmate named Mansfield B. Frazier reveals the nature of the modern American inferno and thus the central issues of our criminal justice system from an angle often ignored by those who are outside the walls of prison.[36] We learn about the wages of racism and its lingering effects within the very system of justice commissioned to eradicate it. Frazier steps into the innermost circle of America's beleaguered underclass and sojourns in the dismal land inhabited by those who are now part of our incarcerated subculture. Frazier has been arrested fifteen times on felony charges and convicted five times. His sentences have been served throughout the United States. He is currently incarcerated at the Federal Correction Institution at Ashland, Kentucky. Frazier's description and reflection on race and criminal justice ends with advice and admonitions. Not content to leave us despairing, Frazier offers reasoned solutions to the problems accounting for our seemingly unstoppable spiral toward inner-city anarchy. His is a voice that speaks out of the agony and pain of incarceration, speech brought out of pain and bewailing. To see hope restored to those corners of America where it has long been presumed extinct; to offer practical and potentially successful means of dealing with the problems of crime and drug use; and to encourage a rapprochement between alienated groups in American society: these are Mansfield Frazier's ultimate ambitions in *From Behind the Wall*. His truth-telling is that no race has ever advanced into the position of health and well-being piecemeal, with half moving ahead and the other half falling further behind:

> The black middle class at last realizes no amount of education or hard work will guarantee career success in white corporate America and the only road to real success must be the one which lifts up the race as a whole. The conclusion they are making is that they, more than any-one else, are responsible for assuring that the one-third of their race mired in poverty doesn't remain there. Finally, and maybe most importantly, the continued downward spiral of the underclass has awakened the body politic to the fact that new methods have to be developed if we are serious about eliminating the pockets of poverty in this land of plenty. We are all suffering too much from the crime these conditions breed.[37]

His voice is the pain of the criminal justice system brought to speech and made available to us as the mediator of a new imagination. This society can no longer afford to be exclusive in its desire for well-being. It has to extend the desired goal to include the poor, the criminal, the entire underclass. It is the public cry of pain that has been the engine of energy for a new way of understanding criminal justice in our society. The cry of pain focuses energy and identifies truth at the margins of our society. "It will do us little good to win full equality only to die from a poisoned environment."[38]

"We Shall Not Be Moved"—Neighbors as the Proximate Source of Hope: Life of Appreciation and Not of Devaluation and Manipulation

"If only it were all so simple! If only there were evil people somewhere committing evil deeds, and it were necessary only to separate them from the rest of us and destroy them. But the line dividing good and evil cuts through the heart of every human being. And who is willing to destroy a piece of his own heart?"[39] Aleksandr Solzhenitsyn's words about evil also speak of the evil of racism. The seldom-stated but deeply shared need in our society to maintain people of color in a subordinate position serves to maintain stability and solidarity among the dominant racial population, whose own social and economic status varies widely. As a result, progress in efforts to gain racial equality is so hard to achieve and so easy to lose precisely because rights for people of color are always vulnerable to sacrifice to further the needs of the dominant racial group. Initially, "outsiders" are created in order to have a monopoly from which some are excluded. This monopoly of power is readily translated into a monopoly of sanctity and virtue. In American society, there is an intense sorting out of what is acceptable and unacceptable, the unacceptable being categories treated as morally inferior, socially dangerous, and existentially marginalized. We must address the reality that we live in a society in which racism has been internalized and institutionalized and is woven deeply into a culture from whose inception racial discrimination has been a regulative force for maintaining stability and growth and for maximizing other cultural values. Racism is the manifestation of the deeply entrenched determination to maintain the existing dominant culture and group. Only a full awareness of this disturbing reality leads to a new insight into what is possible. "The nation cannot redeem what has not been established." This is neither a prescription for despair nor a counsel of surrender but is a necessary precondition for a new vision of human relatedness.

A strange and curious thing is that the racially devalued, excluded from the dominant group, do not respect boundaries set in society. They cross them in desperate quest of the necessities of life. Those who are categorized as "outsider" and "stranger" do not stay perpetually consigned to that role and identity. Out of their displaced vantage point comes a wisdom that they can no longer afford to be exclusive in their quest for their rights. They have to include both other disadvantaged groups and the oppressors as well. The wisdom is to raise a new generation of people who are not confined by narrow self-interest but are prepared to lead the whole society to a brighter tomorrow. There is an unsettling that unnerves, threatens, and sometimes undoes the dominating system, an unsettling that effects an inclusion of the outsider, a welcoming of the stranger, and the practice of hospitality within a system of vengeance and fear. The gift of power for life given outside the control of the dominating group depends on the devalued bringing hurt, hate, and grief to public speech in the midst of a community, as Walter Brueggemann reminds us. Public sharing of pain and bewailing is the means whereby power and courage well up among the devalued. As long as the racially vulnerable and devalued docilely accept the status of victim or believe that the status assigned by the prevailing power is a fixed fate, nothing transformative or redemptive will happen. The monopoly will continue its crushing, preemptive force as long as silence can be enforced. The cry of protest and anguish is a daring, courageous assertion that this unequal arrangement is not right, will not be accepted or tolerated, and must be changed. In the moment of such a bewailing and of shrill speech, the dominating system is disclosed as a fraud that does not keep its promises and is not what it claims to be. In that dangerous moment of the cry, it is clear that the system is not the solution, but is in fact a large, painful problem. The cry insists that the dominating group must negotiate with a party that it does not even recognize as existing, even if the dominating group's goal is its own well-being. To paraphrase the words of Mansfield Frazier, it will do one little good to attain one's well-being only to die from a poisoned environment. The cry asserts that "we" are here as a serious social reality that cannot be pretended away. "However I am perceived and deceived, however my ignorance and conceits, lay aside your fears that I will be undone, for I shall not be moved," says Maya Angelou. "I would submit that a nation cannot restore what it has not established," says Benjamin E. Mays. Vision breaks through brokenness. There voices are signs of hope. These signs come from subsidiary institutions in society, where neighbors come together, where different expressions of imagination are born that counter the monopoly of imagination and power, where neighbors serve as the proximate source of hope. Abraham Heschel says: "Fellowship depends upon appreciation, while manipulation is the cause of alienation: objects and I apart, things stand dead. . . . I am alone. . . . Reality is equated with availability; what I can manipulate is, what I cannot manipulate is not. A life of manipulation is the death of transcendence."[40] The voices of neighbors in subsidiary institutions bespeak a wistful longing for another life that could be lived with a singleness of vision that is driven by neither rage nor fear. These voices invite a faithful living-through. That living-through is possible, however, only when the pathos of personhood, the rawness of power, and the hidden resilience of human hope converge. These neighbors strive to express in their living this faithful living-through. We will hear these voices in the next chapter.

dominant and underrepresented racial groups. [We have not been able to create a positive alternative vision and new possibilities powerful enough to move hearts, create communities, and generate new and powerful subcultures with shared values,] common processes of evaluation, and regularities of behavior. The deep pain of racial plurality prevails today. Race indeed matters because race is inseparable from our societal identity. There is literally nothing in the American identity that does not partake of its quotient of color. Matters of race for us afford a disciplined teaching of our own insights into our shared human conditions, our peoplehood. There is a fullness, even a richness amid the pain of our racial estrangement. Where can we locate sources of regeneration for the sake of all of us who need visions of human possibility that transcend the dividing walls of hostility?

Before we respond, we need to acknowledge that this way of posing the question is itself based on a particular way of experiencing and reading the racial scene in the United States that is not always commonly supported. Two traditions, one optimistic and the other pessimistic, have coexisted on the fiendishly complicated question of race. There are those who argue that our current obsession with race will eventually wither away amid increasing racial blurring and continued enforcement of progressive social policies. Stephen and Abigail Thernstrom, for example, maintain that the United States has gone a long way in the past six decades toward eliminating the stain of racism from the white American heart.[2] Stanley Crouch also argues that in the future definition by racial, ethnic, and sexual groups will most probably have ceased to be the foundation of special-interest power. In our present love of the mutually exclusive, and our pretense that we are something less than a culturally miscegenated people, Crouch says, we forget our tendency to seek out the exotic until it becomes a basic cultural taste, the way pizza or sushi or tacos have become ordinary fare.[3] This view guarantees that "those who live on this soil a century from now will see and accept many, many manifestations of cultural mixings and additions."[4] Such a reading of the future of race in America assumes that our identities are not fixed in a binary opposition: black-white, native-foreign, ourselves-other. Ralph Ellison describes a young, light-skinned, blue-eyed, Afro-American–featured individual who could have been taken for anything from a sun-tinged white Anglo-Saxon to an Egyptian or a mixed-breed American Indian.[5] Too often we create our identities within fragilely constructed oppositions that flimsily disguise the fears of inadequacy and failure that nag at us. The challenge, Ellison says, is that of arriving at an adequate definition of American cultural identity.

Those who hold an optimistic view of race argue that eventually we will come to an understanding that our similarities do not disempower us, but rather create a profound synergy. We all belong to several communities at once, and these multiple memberships often reflect corresponding interests and goals. Consequently, focusing on the common interests of communities in order to form coalitions dedicated to cooperative action offers the best strategy for social and political change. One hundred years from today, they argue, Americans are likely to look back on the ethnic difficulties of our time as quizzically as we look at earlier periods of human history when misapprehension defined the reality.[7]

A derivative reading of the optimistic tradition is that of Robert Bellah et al. who argue that our society is divided not so much by race but by deepening class divisions: "we believe that it is not so much race discrimination that is the problem, though that continues to be serious enough, but, rather, the racialization of the class hierarchy—the Balkanization of America."[8] This group believes that race differences are real but they should not obscure how much we have in common. Both the dominant Anglo-European Americans and Americans of color share most of the ideology of the American dream, not only material but moral aspirations. By focusing exclusively on race differences, they argue, we tend to obscure the fact that race differences are rooted in class differences. "Class differences transcend race and divide all Americans." Based on their previous works, *Habits of the Heart* and *The Good Society,* which warned of the dangers of unchecked individualism in the American character, they argue that their warning went unheeded and that the consequences manifest themselves in the economic stratification of this society undermining the sense of community. "Community" is defined as solidarity with neighbors, both near and far, who share a sense of connection, destiny, and mutual responsibility. Underlying this definition is the view that individuals live in a society that has a common good beyond the sum of individual goods and that individuals thrive fully only when rooted in communities that transcend individual concerns. But "the house today is divided . . . by deepening class divisions. . . . Class differences transcend race and divide all Americans."[10]

And yet, making class a proxy for race turns out to be wrong-headed under careful examination, particularly at the policy-making level of our government.[11] The current debate on affirmative action is a case in point. Preferences based on socioeconomic class and race are not interchangeable. They address distinct forms of disadvantage. Class preferences are designed to help the poor of any race. Race preferences are designed to help people of color of all classes. Both are necessary and valid forms of preference, but one cannot substitute for the other. Having examined the Asian American students' admissions into the California state university system, Dana Y. Takagi poses the question: "Given the problems of shifting from race to economic class in reforming affirmative action, why are people pressing the idea?" At least one answer is that the conservative policy makers and their supporters know that changing to class will not benefit people of color and that they believe the time is over for granting any special treatment to people of color. Ours is a society that still does not offer equal opportunity to all its citizens. Policies that help diminish class divisions as well as race divisions can be an important step toward social equality. But substituting class for race in social policy is just not adequate to the challenges we face.

This is still a nation living on opposing and often adversarial sides of a yawning racial divide. We need to acknowledge the reality of American racism deeply woven into our social matrix in order to talk constructively about race relations. Only a full awareness of the reality of racism ripens our wisdom. We need to honestly face the unavoidable and painful truth that this nation's social stability is historically built on the belief in and the determination to maintain the dominance of a particular group, Anglo-European Americans, who established the nation. Racism is the manifestation of this deeply entrenched determination. Even a total reform of our economy and other social systems would not erase and might even intensify the need of the dominant group to measure their self-worth by maintaining people of color in a subordinate status. It is true that we live in an era of increasingly blurred lines of racial identity. There is indeed an illusion of precision about race. There are voices that speak of an irrelevance of racism in the matrix of our shifting identities and optimistically about the future of race relations: "I am fairly sure that race, as we currently obsess over it, will cease to mean as much 100 years from today," one such voice says.[12] But such an optimistic reading of human relationships does not sufficiently acknowledge the deeply ingrained propensity to evil that accompanies our race relations. Color is seen as being "less" human. If only it were all so simple! Augustine, Buber, Solzhenitsyn, and a score of wise voices remind us that we do not have certain evil people somewhere committing evil deeds and we need only separate them from the rest of us and destroy them. "But the line dividing good and evil cuts through the heart of every human being. And who is willing to destroy a piece of [their] own heart?"[13] Applying this reading of evil to our race relations is neither a prescription for despair nor a counsel of surrender, but it does carry risks. The acknowledgment of the presence of evil within us personally and societally is a condition for responsibility. Creativity flowing from such an acknowledgment serves to lift the weight of the hopelessness and cynicism that accompany denial. We still ask: If racial subordination is inevitable in our relationships, and if all our efforts and accomplishments will come to little, then what is the use of working for racial justice and the reestablishment of just and equitable relations among racial groups?

A response to the question calls for more than sociological or political readings of race relations. It leads us into the realm of fear, distrust, and deeply held convictions that have been formed over many generations. Only when we honestly ask the question are we directly facing the unstated truth that has bedeviled us all along: ours is a society in which one's identity, personal or group, is governed by fear, suspicion, and violence. This seething brutality is at work right beneath the surface of our public life. We are less likely to trust those who are different, whose values are unfamiliar, and whose skin color is dark. A thirst to undermine and at times destroy those who are different in order to keep control is at the core of our cultural forces. We find it extremely difficult to be liberated from the fear of "other" people. We find it very difficult to acknowledge our unwillingness to be freed from our own fear. Once the fear is out in the open, we can look at the imprisoned state of life honestly and without illusion. Such honesty is a precondition for engagement and commitment to a caring life, that is, an alternative way of relating across racial lines.

Engagement and commitment connote action and service. The genuine act of reaching out requires humility. Once we recognize and acknowledge our life of enslavement to fear of those who are different and our wish to maintain distance from them, even by violent means, that realization can lead to actions that are less likely to worsen race relations and perhaps may move us into mutually respectful relationships.[14] Such is a perspective from which to gauge the present and future worth of our race-related activities. It is time that we face up to just how difficult it will be to have a positive effect on this country's continuing racial struggle. Those difficulties need not deter us but should give us a basis for a more realistic understanding of what is possible. Any signs of hope we seek in our highly racialized culture of opposition must take into account the difficulty of achieving a vision of a society that is "indivisible, with liberty and justice for all." Where are the signs of just and realistic repeopling? With a sober realization of the reality of race relations we will seek to answer this question as people who confess Christ as the plumb line of life and find in Christian faith communities the locus of a vision of life where "there is neither Jew nor gentile, neither male nor female."

Signs of Repeopling in Christian Churches

Woven into the fabric of Christian faith is the confession that diversity is not a curse, not some problem to be solved, but rather it is the supreme expression of the creative spirit of God. God's self-revelation in Jesus Christ brings into existence a community, the church, which is called and empowered to witness to God's intended wholeness for all creation, God's reign, which is a "domination-free life."[15] In this confession is a realization that we cannot be saved apart from each other, that we cannot separate our lives because we stand next to each other even in our desire to be alone. Moreover, fear, distrust, and hatred of our neighbors return to haunt those who harbor them. Life cannot be lived in separation and isolation. The church's ministry, then, is to witness in its own life and society a vision of life that transcends those barriers that divide persons from one another. Our baptism into Christ and our celebration of his presence at the Table mark us as people whose shared experience of grace is stronger than any dissimilarities among us. This is the vision of the church's essential nature toward which we live, and thus it is the measure by which our life as church is judged. The embodiment of God's reign in this community, the church, is meaningful precisely because it comprises the full diversity of peoples, cultures, traditions, races, and languages. Contrary to prevailing ways of defining people by a particular racial/ethnic identity, gender, language, and culture—that is to say, by the ways we differ from others—Christian faith communities are defined without a common language or racial and ethnic identity. We are tied together not by our own blood, but by Christ's blood.

This new community "in Christ" of those who come from all walks of life, particularly those whom we consider "strangers," is not just the usual way of providing relationships or carrying out mission. The church, when it is true to its essential nature, is a visible embodiment of the good news itself. This means to proclaim, "Love is the way," love without violence, love without reprisals even in the midst of various expressions of human viciousness. To witness to this reality calls for something more than a functional and utilitarian approach to life governed by measurable morality, managerial possibility, and optional ethics. Unlike the conventional law of human groupings that particular identities are cherished and polemically defended even by destroying lives, the starting point of Christian faith community is the wholeness of creation. The starting point is not to find ways of uniting people divided by fear and violence, but to recognize, celebrate, and learn from God's gift of one creation embodied in varied cultures, languages, religions, and races. It is to restore moral integrity in the midst of the culture of decay by restoring freedom and dignity to the captives we held. Our unity in Christ is not an option, but the reality of life by which we are measured. The unity we are given in Christ is meaningful precisely because it comprises the full diversity of peoples, cultures, races, traditions, and languages. We entrust ourselves to this gift of God. What governs our relationship is not the fear of division, but the love of God that says yes to the wholeness of the creation and peoplehood. This is what makes the metaphor for the church in our faith heritage—people of God—so distinct. Peoples are generally defined by language, race, or ethnicity. Contrary to this view of human identity, our faith heritage calls for a peculiar way of defining people—without racial, cultural, gender, or national boundaries but nonetheless related by blood.

Unfortunately, this way of defining human identity is becoming almost inconceivable and is perceived as outrageous and dreamlike in our age. And yet, this reading is precisely the character of our faith perspective on humanity and our relationships one with another. Christians know themselves to be the recipients of such an inconceivable power of being related to each other, which finds its deepest expression of God's grace "in that while we yet were sinners Christ died for us." The church is the community of those who respond to this gracious generosity of God by "welcoming one another as Christ has welcomed us." Such a response takes the form of humanizing an intractable world cowed by the awesome possibilities of continuing walls dividing people, a world where faith wavers and hope stands stagnant. The question for us is: Where can we indeed witness to the signs of this peculiar way of human relationship in a society that continues to keep us enslaved to fear of "others" and violence in race relations?

Before we turn our attention to the signs of hope for the future of race relations in the United States, we need to acknowledge that churches, too, are very much woven into the fabric of racialized America and have been participating in the sin of racism. The history of Christian churches in the United States is no less than a microcosm of our large societal life. How have Christian faith communities responded to the question of what constitutes "we" in today's society in light of race and ethnicity? Christian churches are indeed "in a world," actively participating and deeply enmeshed in the ways life is lived by all people. Only when we are honest about the reality of the life of Christian faith communities can we begin to witness to the genuine signs of hope that move us beyond the impasse in race relations.

Race and ethnicity "in American historiography has remained something of a family scandal, to be kept a dark secret or explained away," says Rudolph J. Vecoli.[16] Based on this image of race, historian Martin Marty comments: "This suggests two dictionary images. One is that of 'a skeleton in the closet,' which is 'a secret source of shame or pain to a family or person.' The other is that of 'a skeleton at the banquet,' a 'reminder of serious or saddening things in the midst of enjoyment.' Equally seriously, ethnicity is the skeleton of religion in America because it provides 'the supporting framework,' 'the bare outlines or main features,' of American religion."[17] The issues of race and racism in Christian churches may well serve as a new occasion for a reexamination of the assumptions and often hidden biases of race relations in the United States.

"The clue to American values, including religious values inso-far as they can be separated, must . . . be sought in the American revolutionary tradition," argues Sydney Ahlstrom.[18] "The funda-mental elements in this libertarian social system were democra-tic government, the Bill of Rights, a free economic order and the security of property. This was a body of thought whose most rel-evant origins can be traced to the leading Puritan theologians and social thinkers."[19] Sadly, the egalitarian principles of the Declaration of Independence, which to a significant extent arose out of Protestant religious values, have been negated in the actual history of American churches. This nation had a chance to rid itself of the scourge of slavery by excluding that most bar-barous abomination from the new nation that the Founders determined to fashion on the high principles of human equality, with liberty and justice for all. The choice ought to have been to use that occasion to affirm our own moral integrity by restoring freedom and dignity to the captives we held. Instead, we chose a meaner path, and the insistent rhetoric about liberty and freedom and justice—like the commitment to nationhood under God—rang hollow against the pitiful cries of the people whose freedom never reached the agenda of serious deliberation except to be judged three-fifths human. The history of racially and ethnically formed churches reveals that these churches are indeed a prod-uct of the refusal of this nation to accept the very values their theological leaders created, namely the rights and privileges that the Declaration of Independence and the Constitution were designed to guarantee to all citizens.

In the face of the continuing reality that eleven o'clock on Sunday morning is the most segregated hour in our society, racially grouped churches continue to engage in a threefold task: (1) to seek access to full rights of peoplehood that are not accorded in a wider society; (2) to confront the apostasy of the racially dominant religious establishment with respect to the unity of the church and the prayer of Christ that the faithful "all may be one"; and (3) to control their own group destiny. If we ask how North American religious values are related to the negation of the very values of dignity, respect, connectedness, and belonging so deeply cherished by racially grouped churches, then "one must acknowledge that [the churches of the dominant racial groups] have been powerfully supportive rather than critical" of the dominant religious establishment in their act of negation.[20]

"To a remarkable degree these ideological attitudes arose out of the Anglo-American Puritan movement; and during the whole course of American history the American Protestant quasi-establishment provided it with divine sanctions." Protestant churches of the dominant racial groups in particular have served a primarily legitimating function for the consistent negation of the egalitarian premise of the Declaration of Independence. One might have hoped that the ideological attitudes might have produced some important Christian response to the ills of society. That the churches had, in fact, provided leadership was widely believed. However, the Christian churches abjectly failed to defend human rights. Christian churches have consistently failed to support, among other things, the admission of Jewish refugees to the United States before, during, and even after World War II. They did not condemn racial segregation, nor did they protest the wholesale imprisonment of Japanese Americans.[21]

The racially dominant churches have often excluded people of color from the dialectics of freedom. Whether people of color will wait for churches to confirm the incongruity of their deeply held values of equality and freedom with the actuality of the negation of these very values in practice is not yet known. But one thing is clear: this incongruity of rhetoric and action deeply ingrained in the history of churches in the United States continues to erode these churches' credibility both for the society as a whole and within their own communities. This incongruity has created a malignancy both within and without the communities of faith that cannot wait for a gradual and self-interested therapeutic solution. The dominant Protestant establishment is the church of the privileged and reflects the values of the privileged. Since the main function of the privileged is to protect the mores of its own class, the solution lies elsewhere.

We need to be reminded by Reinhold Niebuhr, however, that "the fact that [people] can do nothing constructive is no indication of the fact that nothing is being done."[22] What appears obvious sometimes camouflages forces that operate below the level of the visible and consciousness. Where are the signs of such a change? Who is challenging the enduring adversary culture that persists in society? The power and privilege that derive from membership in the dominant culture inflict a myopia that makes it difficult to have a comparable sense of the tribal identity of people of color. A nation indeed cannot restore what has not been established. What is needed is a new angle of vision emerging from the vantage point of those who are not subjected to the myopia of racial and cultural superiority. We also need to be reminded that whatever insight or vision we find in regard to race relations in the United States will not likely make a sweeping change in the current racial scene bound by violence, fear, and death but will likely serve as a reminder of what is possible for us both at present and in the future. Such an angle of vision is the reminder the psalmist gave to all of us amid a variety of life orientations that the affliction of life is still "light enough" in God's sight (Psalm 139).

The Emergence of Peoplehood and the Recovery of Speech

The emergence of a new peoplehood cannot begin in a setting where voices are both familiar and soothing. It begins with the recovery of voices that have been silenced and the vision of life long forgotten. The alienation of people one from another has resulted in an absence of conversation, a loss of speech and sight. In the absence of speech, life is reduced to silence; with the loss of sight, ignorance and fear govern life. "Where there is theological silence, human life withers and dies. Where there is theological silence, blessed communion is impossible."[23] Indeed "communion is not possible where speech is destroyed either by selfishness or by submissiveness" and our sight reduced by myopia.[24] The acknowledgment of theological silence and myopia is a prior task before we can begin to acknowledge the signs of a new peoplehood.

[A new peoplehood emerges as lost voices that have been both silenced and distorted recapture themselves, and their insights into life are regained and publicly heard.]We are once again reminded that though such a statement is easily made, the task is by no means simple and easy. Recovery of speech and sight requires an incredible tenacity on the part of those who are engaged in the task, and its outcome is by no means certain. It is indeed an act of "hope against hope" for those whose voices have long been silenced and their eyes blindfolded. No assurance of receptivity and openness is present on the part of those who have long been accustomed to an old way of hearing and seeing. Often resistance, hostility, and suspicion are expected responses to unfamiliar voices. Nevertheless, the task needs to be carried out.

Voices of the pain and bewailing of devalued people well up and cannot be readily contained. These voices are truth-telling. The task is in this sense an act of faith. Its driving force is no less than faithfulness to grace given and experienced by the neglected. The silenced voices would reclaim themselves not through the message delivered by the prevailing culture, but through the truth authenticated in the experience of suffering in order to reinforce an ingrained religious temperament and to produce an indigenous religion oriented to freedom and human well-being. Signs of new peoplehood emerge from these silenced voices, and the parameter of mutual openness to change is intrinsically a matter of praxis that needs to be engaged by the historically dominant voices as well as the silenced.

Redemptive Traditions

In the context of the North American racial scene, a curious note has entered into our understanding of human relatedness. What happens when the web of humanity is torn asunder by cross-racial estrangement in a society whose relational dynamic is largely based on domination and subjugation? To reflect on this matter is to encounter what for many is a startling disclosure of an insight that is anything but self-evident. "What is remarkable, heartening and humbling to me, is that so many of the oppressed persist in looking for new societies built on forgiveness rather than revenge," remarks Haddon Willmer.[25] The power to witness to the basic relatedness of humanity, peoplehood, has been demonstrated repeatedly throughout history by those who are both devalued and ignored by a dominant group. "Redemptive tradition" is the familiar term within African American faith communities for witnessing to the fullness of humanity, but the tradition is also embraced by other groups of people:

> I know what it is like to be powerless to forgive. That is why I would never say to someone 'You must forgive.' I would not dare . . . I can only say: however much we have been wronged, however justified our hatred, if we cherish it, it will poison us. Hatred is a devil to be cast out, and we must pray for the power to forgive, for it is in forgiving our enemies that we are healed.[26]

Hatred destroys the soul, and no matter how deserving of revenge the oppressor may be, to continue to carry the desire for vengeance is simply to dwell on one's own rage. Forgiveness frees people from the crushing weight of a rage that could consume them. For their own sakes they need to forgive, so that their souls become free of the power of the past to consume them, beyond the power of the oppressor to continue to dominate their minds. But, such desire to be freed from the bondage of hate is not the only reason for forgiveness. The summons to forgive ultimately comes from outside one's own desire. It comes as a command of the gospel as the source of the *raison d'etre* of faith communities. Forgiveness is the fundamental form of faithfulness to God.

Vincent Harding recounts a demonstration of the power of forgiveness as he tells the story of "Coloured People's Convention at

the Zion Presbyterian Church" in Charleston, South Carolina, in
November 1865. Over two thousand freed slaves attended the
convention and made an "Address to the White Inhabitants of
the State of South Carolina."

> What manner of men and women were these? Refusing
> to flinch in the face of the past, attacking the criminal
> system which had bound them, they extended the "right
> hand of fellowship"—a distinctly Christian phrasing—to
> the former criminals, offering to build together a new soci-
> ety. Who were these prophets and potential lovers who
> came to the convention in work clothes and uniforms,
> wrapped their hair in bright turbans and bandannas, and
> made Zion Church a precinct of sanctified hope?[27]

The people of the Zion Presbyterian Church evidenced an ability
to shake free of the revenge, the resentment, the sheer hostility
that slavery must have stirred up in them.

More recently, in June 1996, historic Matthews-Murkland
Presbyterian Church in Charlotte, North Carolina, was destroyed
by arson. It was one of a series of church burnings during the past
several years at mostly Southern black churches. The blaze, which
burned the sanctuary to the ground, was said to have been set by
a disturbed white teenage girl. During a powerful worship service
on the first anniversary of the burning of the church, Presbyterian
leaders announced the establishment of the Hawkins-Buchanan
Fund for Racial Justice and led the denomination of the
Presbyterian Church (USA) in affirming its historic commitment
to racial justice and reconciliation.[28] The grief and pain of the
people of the Matthews-Murkland church are intense. But they
did not let the tragedy change them into something different
from who they are. They are determined to be human.[29]

"Is there, in the culture of black Americans, a predisposition,
an ingrained gift, for injecting the forgiveness of sins into their
political negotiations with us, their white American neighbors?"
asks Donald Shriver Jr.[30] Such an act is the "redemptive tradition"

deeply ingrained and continues to be practiced within African American religious life, a Christian willingness to show mercy rather than condemnation. The redemptive tradition is expressed simply by Martin Luther King Jr. and Mahatma Gandhi before him, who supposedly commented: "An eye for an eye and a tooth for a tooth will leave the whole world toothless and blind." It comes out of the wisdom that the destruction of the "enemy," as tempting as this might be, will merely cause hatred in the enemy's sons and daughters, who will rise up to fight, and if not them, their later generations. The only way to destroy the enemy is to turn the enemy into a friend.

Another redemptive tradition is witnessed within the Native Hawaiian Christian community. The Native Hawaiian Christians proclaim that struggle for *racial* rights is at the same time a struggle for *human* rights. As with the civil rights struggles of the 1950s and 1960s, the less publicized struggle of the Hawaiian *kanaka maoli* (indigenous population) is a struggle for the dignity and diversity of all within the Hawaiian context. "To us *kanaka maoli*, it means *lokahi* (oneness) and *pono* (harmony) with ourselves, each other and all in our cosmos, who represent *kinolau* (many forms) of the great spiritual forces," declares Richard Kekuni Blaisdell of the Pro-Hawaiian Sovereignty Working Group.[31] The struggle of the *kanaka maoli* is that they have no choice but to live as groups in the midst of the entrenched majority cultures—Anglo-European American, Japanese, and Chinese—that sublimate their own diversity of group origins in favor of a received individualist tradition. *Lokahi* and *pono* are spiritual in character: the heritage of a group intrinsically and pervasively involves the passion for a genuine and radical affirmation of all even in the midst of the painful oppressive society.

If justice is understood as righting a wrong, then it is not seen as a precondition to reconciliation in the witnesses of these communities. The reconciling acts of these faith communities are witnesses to the Christian vision of common humanity. These acts serve as a bridge between the past and present society deeply divided by strife, conflict, and untold suffering on the one hand, and a future founded on the recognition of the equality and dignity of all people on the other. To be sure, it is necessary to establish truth in relation to the events. It is equally important to discern the motives for the gross violations of human rights and the circumstances in which they have occurred. These things need to be made known in order to prevent these acts from being repeated in the future. However, the forgiving acts of these communities suggest that there is a deep need for understanding but not vengeance, for reparation but not retaliation, for healing but not victimization of the perpetrators. These forgiving acts point to the hope that brutality and violence in race relations will not happen again. The main ethical issues in these acts relative to the historical process of race relations are truth-telling and reconciliation, not righting the wrong. The important point here is that justice is not the only social goal, nor always the ultimate value. Sometimes we are faced with difficult choices between values. Sometimes we must make judgments about their relative importance. The vision of reconciliation is built upon the faith conviction of the relatedness of all people that is based on being able to come together despite the lack of justice, not because justice is a prerequisite. The vision of reconciliation is based on the power of grace that does not depend on the power of justice. This does not mean that we should ignore the importance of justice or the pain of injustice. But if we are going to seek reconciliation, we need to know that "being fair" does not necessarily create forgiveness and love. Forgiveness depends instead on the acknowledgment of the inherent worth of the "other" in spite of what they have said or done. Forgiveness happens when that worth is recognized.

If the history of African American Christian communities and other Christian communities of color can remind us of their ability to be more hospitable to the forgiveness of America's sins, it also needs to remind us that American culture as a whole has not been receptive to being forgiven. The forgiveness of which our sisters and brothers are capable still waits for a display of a justice of which this society has yet to show itself capable. This power of forgiveness, which was neither demanded nor anticipated by the dominant group and which arose out of the genuine desire of African Americans, Native Hawaiians, and other people of color, is anything but a sentimentalized or intellectual object of observation. Only when this reality of freely offered forgiveness is acknowledged and received with deep appreciation and an awareness of its meaning for self-examination on the evil of racism by the dominant culture can the creation of a true peoplehood—a reconciled, just, and harmonious relationship among diverse groups of people—become possible. Such awareness and self-examination is the first and vital step toward understanding that must be taken if we are to continue as a society together. We must understand the basis upon which we can be a varied people, inhabiting one society with rules and laws that can be used to fulfill expectations of the racial, cultural, social, and spiritual nature of each person within his or her group. Can this society hear and receive such insights coming out of the fringes of our society and from often-neglected and devalued people? This is our true challenge for race relations. Unfortunately, these gestures of forgiveness are often met with suspicion, resistance, and cynicism.

Reconciliation is a clear demonstration of the power and vitality of the Christian faith. It is by restating the challenge of racial reconciliation in the context of the Christian faith that Christians can hope to move toward the vision of justice and mutual relatability, intelligibility, and interdependence. The power to witness to humanity historically, however, lies largely with the underrepresented and oppressed population, not the dominating majority. One of the triumphs of Martin Luther King Jr.'s movement, for example, was its ability to awaken Christians to the power of the gospel and to the uncommon unity that gospel produced. The civil rights movement demonstrated its ability to draw large numbers of Anglo-European Americans and other ethnic Americans into the impassioned fires of the African American religious tradition and, as a consequence, to develop a distinctive form of Christian community. The civil rights movement is essentially a movement of the church that originated in

African American faith communities.[32] The real enemy of the gospel that was routed was not so much Jim Crow but the walls of hostility separating races.

This is to say that the agenda of the civil rights movement still remains alive and unfinished. The challenge race relations pose today is "the faith in the ultimate justice of things," as W. E. B. DuBois articulated, to find *oikos*, community, the basic form of humanity as Christians confess, in the midst of the apparently insurmountable powers of racial division. The challenge before Christians, regardless of their racial identities, is to harness the energy of faith in building communities of justice and truth, mutual accountability and love, communities united by the eucharistic power of the gospel at work in the midst of life. For Christians of color, the challenge is to continue witnessing to the signs of the breaking down of the dividing walls of hostility, no matter how painful and difficult such witness may be. Such witness is the only way we become liberated from the oppositional ways of defining humanity based on fear and violence that prevail. For Christians of the dominant racial group, the task is to receive the gift of such witness from people of color and to reexamine the prevailing pattern of human relationships in light of the gift. The problem has been that people of color have not had a public platform within racist society that enables them to give their pain a hearing and their insights and wisdom a platform for realization in the whole society. The role of the subjugated racial groups in the well-being of the whole society remains the only option for us. Only when this reality of our society is grasped will the reality of peoplehood that is in the Christian practice called eucharistic fellowship become what it has always struggled to be: not a buried insight but a revolutionary power that guides humanity into the future.

The challenge that race relations pose today is that of finding community in the midst of the apparently insurmountable powers of racial division. This challenge is a call for Christians, those of the dominant racial group as well as Christians of color, to harness the energy of the good news in building communities of truth and justice, mutual accountability and love, communities united by the power of the One who brings all humanity together. Racial separatism and isolation are self-defeating. A recent extreme example is the Rwandan situation. The Hutu politicians created a situation from which there is no escape. They have made their opponents into such demons that they have no outs for themselves. There is no way to turn back. The language of extremism appeals to fear; there is no means of negotiation, so they have to discredit their own propaganda. In the United States, the self-destructive nature of racial separatism has also been demonstrated at various points in its history. In 1925, somewhere between twenty-five and forty-five thousand members of the Ku Klux Klan marched from the Capitol, down Pennsylvania Avenue, to the Washington Monument. A. H. Gulledge, of Columbus, Ohio, led the knights and delivered the keynote address. He said that the Klan was motivated not by racial or religious prejudice but merely concerned that "the races remain as God intended they should remain"—segregated. That day, August 8, 1925, turned out to be the Klan's last great day, the high-water mark of white supremacy in the United States. The government rewarded the Klan members who wanted to stand alone by granting them their desire. It was a wise decision. The government permitted the Klan its own wish to be excluded from the emerging religiously, ethnically, and racially mixed America, and that, inexorably, meant the end of the Klan's political power. The reality is that people with various racial identities cannot be saved apart from one another, apart from forming a community across the racial divide. That is the basic source of the vitality of life. We cannot separate our destiny, as seems to be the conventional suburban dream, because we are, even after all this trouble, standing next to each other. This reality is precisely what has been revealed in the Table Fellowship in which Christians participate regularly and which is embodied in the lives of the churches.

The signs of peopling are numerous, though they are often overlooked and the voices of the messengers ignored. From the Plaza United Methodist Church in Charlotte, North Carolina, to

St. Elizabeth Catholic Church in Oakland, California, churches are working toward community building across racial lines. From urban Detroit to rural Kentucky, churches and community-development groups have joined hands to revitalize their neighborhoods and communities as means of fighting entrenched racism in society. The products of these partnerships include affordable housing for the poor and elderly, new jobs, the retention of established businesses, improved social and financial services, and a renewed spirit for improving race relations and racial fragmentation. The goal of these partnerships is to redeem the souls of our society. Their task is to renew the dominating culture and ethos of this society, which has been poisoned by the moral decay of racism. The signs of hope for racial relations are those churches who consider their mission as carrying forward the work of building community across racial barriers even in the midst of the dominant racial churches' capitulation to racial division. Amid the race fatigue caused by the apparent shortcomings of the civil rights movement, along with the disenchantment of those who have attempted to raise its banner in recent years, there are churches that insist that it is only by restating the challenge of racial reconciliation in the context of the gospel that Christians can hope to move forward in breaking down the dividing walls of racial hostility.

Their mission is always daunting. Unlike civil society and the legal environment, people are free to do as they wish in the church, and so people travel more slowly in their freedom than they do when they are legally brought together. Furthermore, unlike Roman Catholics, who are expected to attend their neighborhood parish, Protestants may attend any church, regardless of geography. To complicate the situation, the challenge of breaking down the dividing walls of hostility is about culture as much as race. In addition to racism, an issue of ethos—worship ethos, for example—is involved, one where the spiritual dimension of the church mixes with the cultural. Thus the most segregated time of the week still remains Sunday morning. The real challenge is to effect a change in people's hearts, which cannot be legislated or forced. That is the experience of churches such as Plaza United Methodist Church in Charlotte, North Carolina, and the First United Methodist Church of Jamaica, Queens, in New York City. The roads toward the manifold breakdown of walls of racial hostility have been rocky for these and other churches struggling to meet the challenge. Long emotional power struggles took place in these parishes, involving lay leaders, pastors, and denominational district leaders. Amid painful negotiations and decisions, often resulting in the departure of longtime church members, some signs of hope emerge. For the Plaza United Methodist Church, this hope was expressed by the affirmation of Dr. Percy Reeves, an African American pastor in the traditionally white congregation.[33] For the First United Methodist Church in Queens, New York, one of the first signs of hope was the healing instruction of its pastor, Rev. John Cole, for the parishioners to write down their name and telephone number on a piece of paper, pass it to someone across the aisle, and call that person during the week and ask if he or she needs a prayer. It was a step, though a modest one, toward breaking down the walls of suspicion and fear of its membership, which consists of African Americans, Anglo-European Americans, and immigrants from Africa, Asia, and the Caribbean. It is a step toward healing the wounds that some people may be nursing.

Community revitalization is another expression by faith communities to meet the challenge of reconciliation across racial lines. A variety of churches and church-related organizations, sometimes assisted by funding foundations, have been involved in partnership projects to revitalize neighborhoods. Earlier, the Roman Catholic Campaigns for Human Development and the Presbyterian Self-Development of Peoples Fund, for example, were part of the support that national religious groups have provided. On local levels, African American congregations and the B'nai B'rith were among the earliest and most-active sponsors of affordable housing for the elderly. During the 1980s, religious involvement escalated, partly because of changes in the community-development environment, until government funding became more scarce and more competitive during the Reagan administration. Eventually new efforts of community revitalization began to emerge among private sectors, development banks, loan funds, and financial and technical networks, which came to be called "intermediaries." They were often backed by foundations and corporations and called Community Development Corporations (CDCs). Most of the CDCs have a local focus and a local board of directors. CDCs with religious roots are common. In Detroit, Cass Corridor Neighborhood Development Corporation serves a large area north of downtown where 51 percent of the racially mixed population live below the poverty level. Although independent, the CDC has a long-standing partnership with Cass United Methodist Church.

Known for its long-established history and solid experience is Bethel New Life in the West Garfield Park section of Chicago. Set up by a small Lutheran church in 1979, this agency, now with a staff of more than 150 persons, engages in housing, job creation, job placement, and social services. Bethel New Life built or rehabilitated some 1,300 rental or owner-occupied units. It also established a worker/owner home health-care cooperative, two child-care centers, and several small business and community credit unions in racially diverse and often conflicted neighborhoods on the west side of Chicago.

St. Elizabeth Catholic parish in the largely Latino district of Oakland, California, is involved in an attempt to shape the economic and political life of the community sponsored by the Oakland Community Organization (OCO), a local affiliate of the Pacific Institute for Community Organization (PICO), which coordinates the work of local congregation-based federations in nearly thirty cities nationwide. The purpose of OCO is to work to foster local economic development, including a specific time line for redeveloping the neglected hulk of what was once a Montgomery Ward store. The basic thrust of PICO for its civil engagement is accountability and partnership. "Accountability" means that political leaders agree to meet with and address the community agenda of the PICO membership. Where this accountability is lacking, PICO may still use the old techniques of power politics. But PICO is beginning to develop a "partnership" model, in which dialogue between PICO citizen-leaders and their elected political officials defines a common agenda for city government. "Christianity and politics. In the current political climate, to juxtapose the two words evokes fears that extremist and intolerant elements of American life will impose their views on the wider society. Yet religious commitment has frequently undergirded the most tolerant aspects of American public life, including movements for progressive social reform," says Richard Wood of the University of California at Berkeley.[34]

The participation of churches and other religious groups often brings certain intangible qualities to such community redevelopment projects. Faith communities often provide an opportunity for people to experience and grow, to be volunteers, and to get a clearer view of what it means to relate to one another across racial lines in order to build the sense of community. Rev. Canon Ronald Spann, rector of the Church of the Messiah in Detroit, Michigan, a partner in the Messiah Housing, a CDC project in partnership with the Episcopal Diocese of Michigan, articulates the theological meaning of community. It is a group of people intentionally living in shared space—or next door or around the corner—and dividing all resources. The combination of spiritual renewal and intentional community fosters "a new vision of the church" that allowed "a blending of the pastoral and prophetic vocations."[35] An integral part of what it means to be a community of faith involves enlarging the sense of community beyond the local congregation. People who care for their own well-being become more invested in the community and in taking care of it as well as in having caring relations with their neighbors across racial divides. To become real to each other, in other words, is the theological meaning of community building, that is, peopling.

These signs of peopling in America are present in numerous places even in the midst of the adversarial ways we relate to each other across racial lines. In spite of numerous attempts to improve race relations in recent decades, the basic adversarial pattern of relating across the race lines remains tenaciously intact. Societal sanctions cannot be the primary means of addressing the ontological dimension of race relations. The signs of hope that are present in Christian faith communities reveal this dimension of race relations and, at the same time, the vision of humanity by which the present reality is being measured. The vision speaks of what is possible in race relations. It also provides us with clues as to how race matters and how the challenges are to be addressed. These clues are not merely utilitarian clues about how to solve race issues; rather, they speak of how people are to live with each other.

Conclusion

Twenty-some years ago, the Kerner Commission appointed by President Johnson predicted that this society is fast becoming "two nations," each separate and unequal. Even with significant progress made in regulating racial problems today, we are multiple nations, each more and more divided and estranged by race, ethnicity, class, and their accompanying values and worldviews. The fear of difference and division continues to rule our day. Race is one of the most explosive and divisive issues in the United States. The "basic form of humanity," as Karl Barth called it, is in trouble because it continues to be distorted by the tension of inequality accompanied by violence, brutality, and the thirst for blood. The upheavals that shake our time revolve around this central issue. To be sure, our Constitution assures us of the structural coherence of the republic while providing for the existence of divergence within society. The current threat of societal fragmentation due to inequality, violence, and brutalization arises from the erosion of mutual trust and the increasing suspicion among various groups that have historically arisen out of the devaluation of many by a privileged few. The relational threads that bind various communities together are being torn apart. Alienation across racial lines lies at the heart of our problem. The issue is theological for Christians because the truth-claims embedded in our confessional faith of the unity and integrity of the whole creation are being assaulted. The Christian claim that our communities are indeed "heirs according to promise" necessitates the manifold breakdown of the dividing walls of hostility toward the establishment of a commonly owned peoplehood.

Ralph Ellison's novel *Invisible Man* is one of the indisputable classics of American literature. He understood the oppression of African Americans as an essential and irreducible fact of American life. And yet he also waged an untiring intellectual war against those "who regard blackness as an absolute, and who see in it a release from the complications of the real world."[36] Ellison refused to participate in the emotionally satisfying cult of "black rage" or the reduction of African American people to a category of oppression. He also repudiated all notions of a separate black culture, insisting throughout his life that black identity was inseparable from the American identity. For him, the question is indeed that of a commonly owned peoplehood for Americans. This question is increasingly becoming an urgent question for us all. How does race define people? The words of DuBois are instructive:

> Through all the sorrow of the Sorrow Songs there breathes a hope—a faith in the ultimate justice of things. The minor cadences of despair change often to triumph and calm confidence. Sometimes it is faith in life, sometimes a faith in death, sometimes assurance of boundless justice in some fair world beyond. But whichever it is, the meaning is always clear: that sometime, somewhere, [people] will judge [people] by their souls and not by their skins. Is such a hope justified? Do the Sorrow Songs sing true?[37]

The "Sorrow Songs" are part of the memory that propels Americans into the future of peoplehood. What seems to have been an innocuous vision of the future—the "ultimate justice of things"—now becomes a liberating metaphor that can continue to be read forward into our own situation.

We began this book with the heart of our task in race relations: We need something we do not yet have, a way of speaking about the pain of racial division and alienation that does not falsify the eschatological grounding of our faith; a way of speaking about hope that does not distort the enduring realities of human estrangement. Commonly shared and owned peoplehood is the "ultimate justice of things" in race relations.

The realization of the basic, mutually relational form of humanity—peoplehood—is, however, not a mere dream in today's society. There are signs of promise incarnated in the midst of decay, signs that exist in often unconventional or unnoticed places. The "heirs according to promise" live at the fringes of society. But indeed they exist among us. For them, decay is not an abstraction; it is the concrete reality in the midst of which all life and thought unfold. As we have seen, the signs of promise for reconciliation across the racial divides are often embedded right within a particular racial community and its spiritual tradition. What is common is inductively contained within the particular. Once this wisdom is grasped, the possibility of new, mutual, reciprocating exchanges, each dependent on the other, arises—but it can do so only along the route of an oscillating exchange that begins from the side of the fringe in society.

At the same time, such exchanges are very costly. Martin Luther King Jr. reminded us that "the white liberal must rid himself of the notion that there can be a tensionless transition from the old order of injustice to the new order of justice. Two things are clear to me, and I hope they are clear to white liberals. One is that the Negro cannot achieve emancipation through violent rebellion. The other is that the Negro cannot achieve emancipation by passively waiting for the white race voluntarily to grant it to him."[38] After almost two decades, violence and brutality are still in the forefront of our concerns. Indeed there cannot be a tensionless transition from the old order of injustice to the new order of justice. More than ever before we are confronted with a "chance to choose between chaos and community"—prophetic words spoken almost two decades ago.

America keeps eluding a final definition. Ours continues to be an unfinished society, increasingly diverse in race and ethnicity, the lines becoming even more elusive. And yet racial divisions remain because they are related to the matter of social control. Color blindness leads to further color division. The simple proclamation of the gospel of reconciliation is not enough to effect the liberation of humanity in its basic form. Both the distortion and ruin and the awakening and realization of a multiracial society turn on the reality of the mutually relational form of humanity. The struggle for the rights of a specific group is a struggle for the rights of all. The awakening and realization of multiracial humanity correlates with this. However it is construed, whether at the hands of the gospel or at the hands of any other truth-claim, it must either await or accompany the removal of domination and subjugation to realize its ultimate worth and dignity. An affirmation of our oneness in Christ, no matter how eloquently stated or how poetically woven into the life of the faith communities of color, will not erase the consequences of racism. The racially oppressed have been saying this for centuries. Martin Luther King Jr. in one of his more eloquent moments states the problem this way: "Worship at its best is a social experience with people of all levels of life coming together to realize their oneness and unity under God"—precisely because of the insurmountable nature of racial divisions. Why? Because the worshipers participate in the eschatological yearning of what is yet to come by which we gauge today's pain. Worship is a powerful expression of the tenacity of hope for Christians for the day when dividing walls of hostility will fall. Worship is a defiant expression of hope against hope in the face of the adversarial culture.

Race has long functioned as the supporting framework of churches for Christians of color. For racially underrepresented Christians, churches have served as a cohering center of their racial identities and histories. Self-respect and racial pride are nurtured in the community of faith. Churches are a haven for people of color in the midst of an often hostile and distrustful society. In church both spoken and nonverbal communication take place without the fear of being misunderstood and rejected. Shared values are implicit in relationship and interaction, and it is through these that churches foster and maintain the racial identity of a people. But churches are more than an arena of self-affirmation for people of color. Church gatherings are occasions for reminding them of what is the "ultimate justice of things."

At the same time, whenever the church consciously or unconsciously caters exclusively to one race or class, it loses the spiritual force of the 'welcoming each other' posture and is in danger of becoming little more than "a social club with a thin veneer or religiosity."[39] In the final analysis, the litmus test for the church is not how the church presumes to change a society, but rather how the church will be changed in the process of engagement. If the church does not change, it may well have paid the final installment on its worst nightmare. Nothing is more explosive or destructive for a society than to have major segments of its people convinced that they have nothing more to lose facing another segment convinced that they have everything to lose. We Christians know ourselves to be the recipients of an "inconceivable" love, which finds its deepest expression in that "while we yet were sinners Christ died for us." The church is the community of those who respond to this memory of the future, this unfathomable generosity of God, by welcoming one another as Christ has welcomed us. Such a challenge is truly "the hallowing of the everyday" as Martin Buber commented—the redemption of our evilness through the creation of community in relation with God.

Race indeed matters because it profoundly impacts the fabric of U.S. society at the deepest level. Theologically, the matter of race fundamentally rests on the question of how people relate to each other, particularly those who do not share a common history, and form a community with them. "A [person] is truly saved from the 'one' not by separation but only by being bound up in genuine communion," Martin Buber once reminded us.[40] But being "bound up" in communion comes precisely out of our failure to enter into relation, the thickening and solidifying of the distance among us. Community building is not a result of a wish for reconciliation and connectedness. "Part of what binds us closest together as human beings and makes it true that no one is an island is the knowledge that in another way every one is an island alone. Because to know this is to know that not only deep in you is there a self that longs above all to be known and accepted, but there is also such a self in me, in everyone else the world over," says Frederick Buechner.[41]

The question we posed in the beginning was this: Can we find an alternative way of relating with each other in the midst of an enduring culture of racial opposition in which we live? In spite of our temptation to answer this question affirmatively, what has led us so far is a recognition that a yearning for racial equality is elusive at best. Short of the extreme of a too-bloody revolution, history tells us that any forward step is likely to drive people of color eventually backward, contributing to the myth that membership in the dominant culture guarantees an ultimately successful existence. Attempts to address programmatic social issues of race will no doubt lead to some improvements. But they cannot be the ultimate solution. Even increasingly blurred racial lines still do not erase internalized and institutionalized racism.

Does this mean that we have to give up our efforts? As we have seen, there are signs of hope for the repeopling of society. These signs suggest that the matters of race relations are more than social and programmatic concerns. They are indeed highly spiritual and religious in nature. The question becomes ultimately that of our convictions, worldviews, faith commitments. These signs suggest that the fight against racism continues even in the midst of a permanent racial inequality in this country, in spite of the futility of action. This may sound contradictory, but what it means is that we must learn to survive the unbearable landscape and climate of truth. We are challenged by racial conditions to extract solutions from our survival even as we suffer what is often bottomless despair. But despair in another sense is a powerful avenue to its contrary existence of engagement and commitment.

This engagement and commitment are what the ancestors of people of color did for centuries: carving out a humanity for themselves with absolutely nothing to help save imagination, will, and unbelievable strength and courage, even in the midst of the monopoly of imagination. These are the postures and message of Christian churches of color. The posture these churches have sought and continue to seek is a hard-eyed view of racism as it is. These churches realize with the neglected forebears of this society that the struggle for freedom is, at bottom, a manifestation of the communal and related nature of our humanity, which survives and grows stronger through resistance to oppression even if that oppression is never overcome. The faith these churches uphold is acknowledging the limits within which we human beings must pursue possibilities and, at the same time, calling into being a community whose most conspicuous mark is the cross, a symbol of the reality that insists that possibilities are given only through the experience of limits; that the way to victory lies through exposure to decay and perhaps death.

NOTES

1. The Spiritual Pain of Interracial Estrangement

1. Henry Louis Gates Jr., "Annals of Race: Thirteen Ways of Looking at a Black Man," *New Yorker,* October 23,1995, 56.

2. See Joseph F. Costanzo, S.J., *This Nation under God* (New York: Herder & Herder, 1964), 29ff.

3. Martin Marty observes that "America as a Protestant culture was a more plausible concept in the thirteen colonies, where not many practiced religion. But the elites who did were Protestant, and they were norm-givers and name-givers in that culture." "The Protestant Experience and Perspective," in *American Religious Values and the Future of America* (Philadelphia: Fortress, 1978), 35.

4. John Adams to Zabdiel Adams, June 21, 1776, quoted in John R. Howe Jr., "Republican Thought and the Political Violence of the 1790s," *American Quarterly* 19, no. 2 (summer 1967): 155.

5. Alasdair MacIntrye describes this well in *After Virtue* (Notre Dame: University of Notre Dame Press, 1981).

6. Quoted in Gates, "Annals of Race," 62.

7. Robert Alter, *The Art of Biblical Poetry* (New York: Basic Books, 1985), 212.

8. Martin Buber, *Between Man and Man,* trans. Ronald Gregor Smith (London: Kegan Paul, 1947/Boston: Beacon Paperback, 1955), 202f.

9. The issue of seeking a way of human relationship that goes beyond the oppositional dynamic that prevails today in the United States is identified by such scholars as Henry Louis Gates, Michael Lerner, and Cornel West. See Henry Louis Gates Jr. and Cornel West, *The Future of the Race* (New York: Alfred A. Knopf, 1996); Michael Lerner and Cornel West, *Jews and Blacks: Let the Healing Begin* (New York: Grosset/Putnam, 1995).

10. The themes of mutual intelligibility, interdependence, and relatability were explored by Benjamin A. Reist in his book *Theology in Red, White, and Black* (Philadelphia: The Westminster Press, 1975). These themes are proleptically suggestive of the direction beyond the current impasse in race relations.

11. Gates and West, *The Future of the Race.*

12. Quoted in Gates, "Annals of Race," 62.

13. Andrew Lam, "The War without End," *San Francisco Chronicle/This World,* April 17, 1994, 8.

14. Ibid., 10.

15. See Robert N. Bellah et al., *Habits of the Heart: Individualism and Commitment in American Life* (Berkeley: University of California Press, 1985).

16. Spencer Perkins and Chris Rice, *More Than Equals: Racial Healing for the Sake of the Gospel* (Downers Grove, Ill.: InterVarsity Press, 1993), 19.

17. Lam, "The War without End," 10.

18. Ibid., 10.

19. Nobu Miyoshi, *Identity Crisis of the Sansei and the Concentration Camp* (Alameda, Calif.: Sansei Legacy Project, 1992), 7.

20. E. G. Satiriko, "The Virtual White Man," *Transpacific* (Malibu, Calif.: April, 1994): 92.

21. "75th Anniversary of Korean Immigration to Hawaii, 1903–1978," edited and compiled by 75th Anniversary Publication Committee (Honolulu, 1978), 50.

22. Satiriko, "The Virtual White Man."

23. McClellan, R. Guy, *The Golden State: A History of the Region West of the Rocky Mountains* (Philadelphia: W. Flint & Co., 1876), 27.

24. Toni Morrison, "The Pain of Being Black," *Time,* May 22, 1988, 36.

25. Ibid., 36.

26. Robert N. Bellah, "The Culture of Contentment and the Underclass: The Making of a Riot," in *Ethics and Policy,* a publication of the Center for Ethics and Social Policy of the Graduate Theological Union, Berkeley, Calif. (summer 1992), 2.

27. Peter Paris, "In the Face of Despair," *The Christian Century* (April 27, 1994): 439.

28. Quoted by Lawrence Wright in "Annals of Politics: One Drop of Blood," *New Yorker,* July 25, 1994, 47.

29. A further delineation of this issue will be given in chapter 2.

30. See Jane Gross and Ronald Smothers, "In Prom Dispute, a Town's Race Divisions Emerge," *New York Times,* August 15, 1994, A10.

31. See Werner Sollors, *Beyond Ethnicity: Consent and Descent in American Culture* (New York: Oxford University Press, 1986).

32. Henry Louis Gates Jr., *Loose Canons: Notes on the Culture Wars* (New York and Oxford: Oxford University Press, 1992), 39.

33. Sau-ling Cynthia Wong, *Reading Asian American Literature: From Necessity to Extravagance* (Princeton, N.J.: Princeton University Press, 1993), 9.

34. Adam Begley, "Colossus among Critics: Harold Bloom," *New York Times Magazine,* September 25, 1994, 32.

35. Ralph Ellison, *The Collected Essays of Ralph Ellison*, ed. John F. Callahan (New York: Modern Library, 1995).

36. Quoted in Isabel Wilkerson in "Whose Side to Take: Women, Outrage, and the Verdict on O.J. Simpson," *New York Times Week in Review,* October 8, 1995.

37. Quoted in the *New York Times,* June 5, 1997.

38. MacIntyre, *After Virtue*, 29–31, 70–75.

39. René Girard, *Violence and the Sacred* (Baltimore: Johns Hopkins University Press, 1977; orig. publication, ed. Bernard Grasset, Paris, 1972).

2. How Does Race Shape People?

1. Quoted from Nadine Gordimer, "Separate," *New York Times Magazine,* June 8, 1997, 48.

2. Ibid., 46

3. Ibid.

4. Max Weber, "Ethnic Groups," trans. Ferdinand Kolegar, in *Theories of Society,* vol. 1, ed. Talcott Parsons et al. (Glencoe, Ill.: Free Press, 1960), 305f.

5. Ibid.

6. George M. Frederickson, *White Supremacy: A Comparative Study in American and South African History* (New York: Oxford University Press, 1981), 153.

7. Ibid.

8. James Ridgeway, *Blood in the Face: The Ku Klux Klan, Aryan Nations, Nazi Skinheads, and the Rise of a New White Culture* (New York: Thunder's Mouth Press, 1990), 79.

9. James A. Aho, *The Politics of Righteousness: Idaho Christian Patriotism* (Seattle: University of Washington Press, 1990),3.

10. In *The Politics of Righteousness,* Aho writes: "The crux of the doctrine is that European Jews are not descended from ancient Hebrew stock at all but from Khazars, residents of a warlike nation of southern Russia who converted to Judaism in the eighth or ninth century. They cannot claim lineage from Abraham, Isaac, and Jacob and are not the covenant people, according to Identity's geneal-ogists. On the contrary, today's Nordic-Anglo-Saxon-Teuton whites are the descendants of the lost tribes of the Biblical Israelites, making white Christians the true people of the covenant. To support this, Hine reinterpreted the book of Genesis with a 'two seed theory.' Eve was seduced by the serpent and bore a son by him, Cain, who slew his brother Abel. After that Adam, the first white man, passed on his seed to another son Seth, who became the father of the white race, God's Chosen People. Cain's descendants, Identity says, are the Jews. They lit-erally are the seed of Satan. Other races, or 'mud people' to racists, descend from others cursed by God." Kevin Flynn and Gary Gerdhardt, *The Silent Brotherhood: Inside America's Racist Underground* (New York: Free Press, 1989), 51.

11. H. Richard Niebuhr, *Christ and Culture* (New York: Harper & Row, 1951), 249–51.

12. Starhawk, in *Women Respond to the Men's Movement: A Feminist Collection*, ed. Kay Leigh Hagan (San Francisco: HarperCollins, 1992), 29.

13. George M. Frederickson's definition of white supremacy is instructive. "Few if any societies that are 'multi-racial' in the sense that they include substantial diversities of physical type among their populations have been free from racial prejudice and discrimination. But white supremacy implies more than that. It suggests systematic and self-conscious efforts to make race or color a qualification for membership in the civil community." *White Supremacy: A Comparative Study in American and South African History* (New York: Oxford University Press, 1981), xi.

14. Jean-Jacques Rousseau, *Discours sur l'origine et les fondemens de l'inegalite parmi les hommes* ("Discourse on the Origin of Human Inequality") (Amsterdam: M. M. Rey, 1755).

15. David Hume, *Essays, Moral and Political* (London: Millar, 1747), 523.

16. Voltaire (François-Marie Arouet), *La philosophie de l'histoire* ("The Philosophy of History") (Geneve: Institut et Musee Voltaire, 1963; New York: Philosophical Library, 1965). Also in *Studies on Voltaire and the Eighteenth Century* (Oxford: Voltaire Foundation, 1990).

17. Johann Friedrich Blumenbach, *De generis humani varietate nativa ("On the Natural Varieties of Mankind")* (Goettigen: Vandenhoeck, 1776). English edition translated and edited by Thomas Bendyshe (New York: Bergman Publishers, 1969).

18. Stephen Steinberg, *The Ethnic Myth: Race, Ethnicity, and Class in America* (Boston: Beacon Press, 1989), 5.

19. Gordimer, *New York Times Magazine*, 46.

20. Robert Blauner, *Racial Oppression in America* (New York: Harper & Row, 1972), 62.

21. Ibid., 63.

22. Gordimer, *New York Times Magazine*, 46.

23. The U.S. Census Bureau Report of 1990.

24. Judy Scales-Trent, *Notes of a White Black Woman: Race, Color, and Community* (University Park: Pennsylvania State University Press, 1995).

25. Colleges hold a special power in shaping Asian American identities. Only 3 percent of the country's population, they represented 5.4 percent of the students in colleges and at universities nationwide in 1994, according to the U.S. Department of Education. It is the only racial group whose percentage of students was above their proportion of the national population.

26. The U.S. Census Bureau Report, May 1997. Lawsuits asserting job discrimination often use statistical evidence from the census to compare the proportion of a particular racial group in a job category with the percentage of that group in a relevant labor pool. Should the use of the multiracial label come into vogue, the total number of, for example, Asian Americans could be reduced, making it more difficult to win some job discrimination cases.

27. Stuart Hall, a professor of sociology at the Open University in London and a founder of what has come to be called cultural studies, argues that ideas

and cultural representations help shape society. Thomas Sowell's *Race and Culture: A World View* (New York: Basic Books, 1994) represents a similar view.

28. Clifford Geertz, quoted in the *Chronicle of Higher Education,* December 14, 1994.

29. Benton Johnson, in his presentation at the Society for the Scientific Study of Religion and the Religious Research Association, November 1996.

30. Ibid.

31. The resolution of the American Anthropological Association, 1994.

32. Luigi Luca Cavalli-Sforza, *The History and Geography of Human Genes* (Princeton, N.J.: Princeton University Press, 1994). Michael Crawford, a professor of biological anthropology at the University of Kansas, came to a similar conclusion. He has collected hair and blood samples from people living near Mountain Altai, a region near Mongolia, in recent years. The subsequent examination of the DNA in those samples proved that the area had been a constant crossroads of human migration. There is no dividing line where on one side it is Asia and on the other side it is Europe, he argues.

33. Sowell, *Race and Culture,* 82.

34. Ibid.

35. Thomas Sowell, *Migrations and Culture: A World View* (New York: Basic Books, 1996).

36. Dinesh D'Souza, *The End of Racism: Principles for a Multiracial Society* (New York: Free Press, 1995).

37. Ibid.

38. Nancy Scheper-Hughes, professor of anthropology, University of California at Berkeley, quoted in the *Chronicle of Higher Education* (December 14, 1994): A18.

39. Cornel West's comment quoted in Karen J. Winkler, "The Significance of Race," *Chronicle of Higher Education* (April 11, 1994).

40. The term "memory of the future" was coined by Letty Russell in her work *Household of Freedom: Authority in Feminist Theology* (Philadelphia: Westminster Press, 1957).

41. See *Reconstructing Christian Theology,* ed. Rebecca S. Chopp and Mark Lewis Taylor (Minneapolis: Fortress Press, 1994).

42. Michael Omi and Howard Winant, *Racial Formation in the United States from the 1960s to the 1980s* (New York: Routledge and Kegan Paul, 1986).

43. Arthur M. Schlesinger Jr., *The Disuniting of America: Reflections on a Multicultural Society* (Knoxville, Tenn.: Whittle Direct Books, 1991).

44. Gates, "Annals of Race," 65.

3. RACISM AS A MONOPOLY OF IMAGINATION

1. The definition of evil as the negation of relationship and the absence of direction is treated best by Martin Buber in *Between Man and Man,* trans. Ronald Gregor Smith (London: Kegan Paul, 1947).

2. Jose Miranda, *Marx and the Bible* (Maryknoll, N.Y.: Orbis Books, 1974).

3. Robert Merton, *Social Theology and Social Structure* (Glencoe, Ill.: Free Press, 1957).

4. Quoted from President Clinton's speech on race in America delivered to graduates of the University of California, San Diego, on June 14, 1997.

5. See John A. Coleman, *An American Strategic Theology* (New York: Paulist Press, 1982).

6. The term is quoted from Archie Smith, *The Relational Self: Ethics and Theology from a Black Church Perspective* (Nashville: Abingdon Press, 1982).

7. Paulo Freire, *The Pedagogy of the Oppressed,* trans. Myra Begman Ramos (New York: Herder & Herder, 1970).

8. Report of Testimony: *Racism in Chicago: A Violation of Human Rights*— Hearings sponsored by the Chicago Interreligious Coalition Against Racism, October 12, 1994.

9. Maya Angelou, from "Our Grandmothers," in *I Shall Not Be Moved* (New York: Random House, 1990).

10. *Racism in Chicago.*

11. William Julius Wilson, "The Ghetto Underclass: Social Science Perspective," in *Annals of the American Academy of Political & Social Science,* vol. 501 (January 1989); Douglass Massey and Nancy Denton, *American Apartheid: Segregation and the Making of the Underclass* (Cambridge: Harvard University Press, 1993).

12. Massey and Denton, *American Apartheid.*

13. Howard E. Freeman et al., "Americans Report on Their Access to Health Care," *Health Affairs* 6 (1987): 6.

14. Sidney D. Watson, "Health Care in the Inner City: Asking the Right Question," 71 *North Carolina Law Review* 1647 (1993).

15. Vernellia R. Randall, "Racist Health Care: Reforming an Unjust Health Care System to Meet the Needs of African-Americans," *Health Matrix* 3 (1993): 127.

16. Elena Nightingale et al., "Apartheid Medicine: Health and Human Rights in South Africa," *Journal of the American Medical Association* 264 (1990).

17. John 14:12: "He who believes in me will also do the works that I do; and greater works than these will he do."

18. *Racism in Chicago.*

19. Michelle Cliff, *Claiming an Identity They Taught Us to Despise* (Watertown, Mass.: Persephone Press, 1980).

20. *Racism in Chicago.*

21. Ibid.

22. Anthony Appiah, "Racisms," in *Anatomy of Racism,* ed. David Goldberg (Minneapolis: University of Minnesota Press, 1990), 3–17.

23. E. San Juan Jr., "Configuring the Filipino Diaspora in the United States," *Diaspora* 3, no. 2 (fall 1994): 117–33; John Beating, "An Appraisal of Functionalist Theories in Relation to Race and Colonial Societies," in *Sociological Theories: Race and Colonialism* (Paris: UNESCO, 1980); "Civil

Rights Issues Facing Asian Americans in the 1990s" (Washington, D.C.: U.S. Commission on Civil Rights, 1992).

24. San Juan, "Configuring the Filipino Diaspora."

25. Bruce Occena, "The Filipino Nationality in the U.S.: An Overview," *Line of March* (1985): 29–41.

26. Ibid., 41.

27. See *Comparative Perspectives on Race Relations,* ed. Melvin Tumin (Boston: Little, Brown, 1969); Melvin Tumin, *Desegregation: Resistance and Readiness,* with assistance of Warren Earnt et al. (Princeton, N.J.: Princeton University Press, 1958).

28. *Racism in Chicago.*

29. Erving Goffman, *Stigma: Notes on the Management of Spoiled Identity* (New York: J. Aronson, 1986).

30. For both African Americans and whites, the level of preparation, as measured by Scholastic Aptitude Test scores, didn't make much difference in who flunked out; low scorers (with combined verbal and quantitative SATs of 800) were no more likely to flunk out than high scorers (with combined SATs of 1,200 to 1,500). The second observation was racial: whereas only 2 to 11 percent of the whites flunked out, 18 to 33 percent of the African Americans flunked out, even at the highest levels of preparation (combined SATs of 1,400).

31. Goffman, *Stigma.*

32. Paul Ricoeur, "Listening to the Parables of Jesus," in *The Philosophy of Paul Ricoeur,* ed. Charles E. Reagan and David Stewart (Boston: Beacon Press, 1978), 245.

33. Randall Kennedy, *Race, Crime, and the Law* (New York: Pantheon, 1997).

34. *Racism in Chicago.*

35. This reading is indebted to Lawrence M. Friedman, in his book *Crime and Punishment in American History* (New York: Basic Books, 1993).

36. Mansfield B. Frazier, *From Behind the Wall: Commentary on Crime, Punishment, Race, and the Underclass by a Prison Inmate* (New York: Paragon House, 1995).

37. Ibid., 248–49.

38. Ibid., 247.

39. Aleksandr Solzhenitsyn, *The Gulag Archipelago, 1918–1956: An Experiment in Literary Investigation,* trans. Thomas P. Whitney (New York: Harper, 1974).

40. Abraham J. Heschel, *Who Is Man?* (Stanford, Calif.: Stanford University Press, 1965), 82–83.

4. Signs of Peopling amid the Adversarial Relationships across the Racial Divide

1. Frederick Jackson Turner quoted in Lee Benson, *Turner and Beard: American Historical Writing Reconsidered* (Glencoe, Ill.: Free Press, 1960).

2. Stephen and Abigail Thernstrom, *America in Black and White* (New York: Simon & Schuster, 1997).

3. Stanley Crouch, "Race Is Over," *New York Times Magazine*, September 29, 1996, 170. Also see his book *All-American Skin Game, Or, The Decoy of Race: The Long and the Short of It, 1990–1994* (New York: Pantheon Books, 1995).

4. Ibid., 171.

5. Ralph Ellison, "The Little Man at Chechaw Station," in *The Collected Essays of Ralph Ellison*, ed. John F. Callahan (New York: Modern Library, 1995).

6. Ibid.

7. Crouch, "Race Is Over."

8. Robert N. Bellah et al., "The House Divided: Meaning and a Renewal of Civic Membership," *Ethics and Policy* (summer 1996): 5.

9. Ibid.

10. Ibid.

11. Dana Y. Takagi, "We Should Not Make Class a Proxy for Race," *Chronicle of Higher Education* (May 5, 1995): A52.

12. Crouch, "Race Is Over," 170.

13. Solzhenitsyn, *Gulag Archipelago*.

14. Derrick Bell, in *Faces at the Bottom of the Well: The Permanence of Racism* (New York: Basic Books, 1992), treats racism from this particular reading of race relations.

15. See Walter Wink's definition of God's reign in *Healing a Nation's Wounds: Reconciliation on the Road to Democracy* (Uppsala, Sweden: Life and Peace Institute, 1997).

16. Rudolph J. Vecoli, "Ethnicity: A Neglected Dimension of American History," in *The State of American History*, ed. Herbert J. Bass (Chicago: Quadrangle, 1970), 70ff.

17. Martin E. Marty, *Religion and Republic: The American Circumstance* (Boston: Beacon Press, 1987), 231.

18. Sydney E. Ahlstrom, "American Religious Values and the Future of America," in *American Religious Values and the Future of America* (Philadelphia: Fortress Press, 1978), 20.

19. Ibid.

20. Ibid., 22.

21. Martin E. Marty, *Modern American Religion: Volume 3: Under God, Indivisible, 1941–1960* (Chicago: University of Chicago Press, 1996).

22. Reinhold H. Niebuhr, "The Grace of Doing Nothing," *Christian Century* (March 23, 1932), 379–80.

23. Walter Brueggemann, *In Man We Trust: The Neglected Side of Biblical Faith* (Atlanta: John Knox Press, 1972), 49.

24. Ibid.

25. Haddon Willmer, University of Leeds, quoted in the *Chronicle of Higher Education* (April 11, 1994).

26. Sheila Cassidy, quoted without reference by D. D. Risher, "The Way to God," in *The Other Side*, no. 31 (Nov.–Dec. 1995), 11.

27. Vincent Harding, *There Is a River: The Black Struggle for Freedom in America* (New York: Harcourt Brace Jovanovich, 1981), 327.

28. *The Racial Ethnic Torch* (Louisville, Ky.: Racial Ethnic Ministries, Presbyterian Church U.S.A.), vol. 9, no. 3 (3d quarter, 1997).

29. Ibid.

30. Donald W. Shriver Jr., *Forgiveness and Politics: The Case of the American Black Civil Rights Movement* (London: SCM Press, 1987), 19.

31. Richard Kekuni Blaisdell, "Martin Luther King and Our Kanaka Maoli Struggle," *Pacific and Asian-American Ministries (PAAM) Newsletter* II, no. 24 (winter 1993): 8 (Cleveland: United Church of Christ).

32. See Perkins and Rice, *More Than Equals.*

33. The story of the Plaza United Methodist Church originally appeared in the *New York Times,* January 2, 1995.

34. An analysis of St. Elizabeth Church's involvement in the PICO project is given in Richard L. Wood, "Communitarianism and Community Organization: Theory Meets Practice," in *Ethics and Policy,* a publication of the Center for Ethics and Social Policy of the Graduate Theological Union (fall 1995).

35. The quote is taken from Linda-Marie Delloff, "Outreach Opportunity Puts Theology in Action," in *Progressions,* a Lilly Endowment Occasional Report (vol. 5, issue 1, February 1995), 6.

36. Ralph Ellison, *Invisible Man* (New York: Vintage Books, 1989).

37. W. E. B. DuBois, *The Souls of Black Folk* (New York: Bantam Books, 1989), 186.

38. Martin Luther King Jr., *Where Do We Go from Here: Chaos or Community?* (Boston: Beacon Press, 1968), 90–91.

39. Coretta Scott King, *The Words of Martin Luther King Jr.* (New York: Newsmaker Press, 1983), 65.

40. Martin Buber, *Between Man and Man,* trans. Ronald Gregor Smith (London: Kegan Paul, 1947), 202f.

41. Frederick Buechner, *Hungering Dark* (New York: Seabury Press, 1968).

INDEX